Collins First School Dictionary

Illustrated by
Stephanie Strickland

Collins

Collins First School Dictionary

First published 2000

This edition published 2005

© HarperCollins*Publishers* Ltd 2005

10 9 8

ISBN-13 978-0-00-720389-5
ISBN-10 0-00-720389-6

A catalogue record for this book is available from the British Library.

Published by Collins
A division of HarperCollins*Publishers* Ltd
77–85 Fulham Palace Road
Hammersmith
London W6 8JB

www.collins.co.uk

Browse the complete Collins Education website at:
www.collinseducation.com

Compilers   Jock Graham, Marie Lister

Literacy consultants   Kay Hiatt, Ginny Lapage
Numeracy consultant   Jan Henley
Science consultant   Rona Wyn Davies

Cover designer   Nicola Croft
Design   Perry Tate Design
Illustrators   Stephanie Strickland,
                Sebastian Quigley (pp. 172–5)

Photos
All commissioned photos by Steve Lumb.

The publishers wish to thank the following for permission to use photographs:
Art Directors & Trip: p. 7 aeroplane, p. 28 castle, p. 59 flower, p. 61 frog, p. 78 jigsaw, p. 94 moon, p. 155 tongue, p. 171 zip; **Biofotos/Heather Angel**: p. 70 hedgehog; **Holt Studios**: p. 23 bud; **ICCE**: p. 49 Earth; **Oxford Scientific Films**: p. 14 badger, p. 27 carrot, p. 60 fossil, p. 63 gerbil, p. 81 koala, p. 87 lizard, p. 105 panda, p. 107 peacock, p. 108 penguin, p. 111 plum, p. 120 raspberries, p. 168 wolf; **Papilio**: p. 6 acorn, p. 8 alligator, p. 10 antelope, p. 16 basket, p. 18 biscuits, p. 19 blackbird, p. 32 cliff, p. 33 coconut; **Tony Stone Images**: p. 12 astronaut, p. 30 chimpanzee, p. 39 crocodile, p. 111 plaster, p. 159 twins, p. 169 wrinkles; **John Walmsley**: p. 144 statue.

All other photos and illustrations © HarperCollins*Publishers* Ltd 2005.

Acknowledgements
The publishers would also like to thank all the teachers, staff and pupils who contributed to this book:

Models

Kayla Castello
Stacey Cleary
Tom Crane
Katherine Davis
William Davis
Nicki Denaro and Mauri-Joy Smith
Elizabeth Fison
Jesse Johnson

Ismael Khan
Lindsay Linehan
Guy Orridge
Zina Patel
Thomas Permaul-Baker
Tom Symonds
Lara Walters

Schools
Aberhill Primary, Fife; ASDAC, Fife; Canning St Primary, Newcastle upon Tyne; Cowgate Primary, Newcastle upon Tyne; Crombie Primary, Fife; Dryden Professional Development Centre, Newcastle upon Tyne; Dunshalt Primary, Fife; Ecton Brook Lower, Northampton; English Martyrs RC Primary, Newcastle upon Tyne; Hotspur Primary, Newcastle upon Tyne; John Betts Primary, London; Lemington First, Newcastle upon Tyne; Literacy Centre, Newcastle upon Tyne; LMTC Education Development Centre, Northumberland; Melcombe Primary, London; Methilhill Primary, Fife; Northampton High, Northampton; Pitcoudie Primary, Fife; Pitreavie Primary, Fife; Ravenswood Primary, Newcastle upon Tyne; St Andrew's CE Primary, London; Simon de Senlis Lower, Northampton; Sinclairtown Primary, Fife; Standens Barn Lower, Northampton; Touch Primary, Fife; Towcester Infants, Northampton; Wooton Primary, Northampton.

Printed by Imago Ltd.

Contents

Using this dictionary

A **dictionary** tells you what a word means and how to spell it. The words in a dictionary are in alphabetical order.

How to find a word

Look for the word "hamster". What letter does it begin with?

guide word | new letter starts here | guide word

alphabet line | headword | definition | alphabet line

You can find the letter "h" in three places:

1 Each new letter starts with **big letters at the top** of the page.

2 Look at the **alphabet line** on the side of the page. This helps you remember alphabetical order, from **a** to **z**. The pink box shows you that the words on this page start with "h".

3 Look at the **guide word** at the top of each page. These are the first and last words on these pages. Here, the first word is "had" and the last word is "have". Do these words start with the same letter as "hamster"?

When you find the right page, look at the blue words. These are called **headwords**. The headwords are in alphabetical order. Find "hamster".

Look at the **definition** under the headword. The definition tells you what the word means.

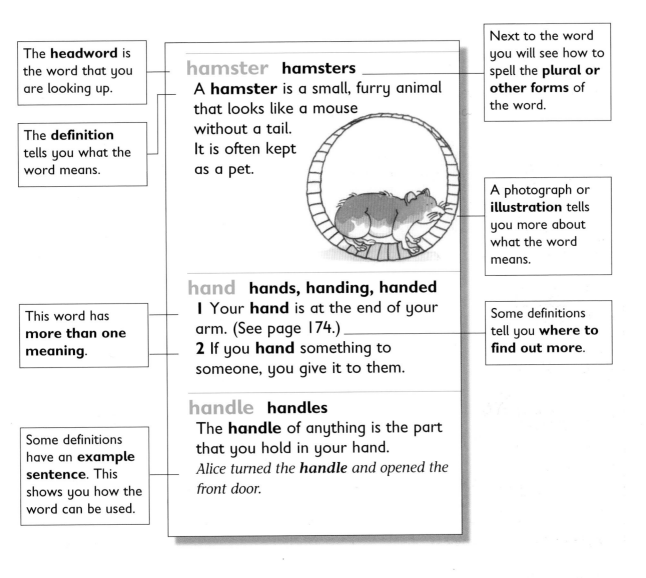

The **headword** is the word that you are looking up.

The **definition** tells you what the word means.

This word has **more than one meaning**.

Some definitions have an **example sentence**. This shows you how the word can be used.

Next to the word you will see how to spell the **plural or other forms** of the word.

A photograph or **illustration** tells you more about what the word means.

Some definitions tell you **where to find out more**.

hamster **hamsters**
A **hamster** is a small, furry animal that looks like a mouse without a tail. It is often kept as a pet.

hand **hands, handing, handed**
1 Your **hand** is at the end of your arm. (See page 174.)
2 If you **hand** something to someone, you give it to them.

handle **handles**
The **handle** of anything is the part that you hold in your hand.
*Alice turned the **handle** and opened the front door.*

Collins Word Wizard

This dictionary also has a special Word Wizard section at the back. It has picture pages, word banks, number banks and games for you to explore.

Picture pages have **illustrations with labels**. Labels tell you what something is called. The labels at the back of this book tell you the names of dinosaurs, parts of the body, parts of a bicycle, parts of a car and clothes.

Word banks and number banks help you learn and spell time words, question words, synonyms and antonyms, shapes and colours.

Aa

b
c
d
e
f
g
h
i
j
k
l
m
n
o
p
q
r
s
t
u
v
w
x
y
z

abacus   abacuses

An **abacus** is a counting frame with beads that move on wires or rods.

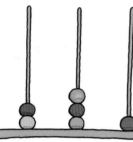

The number of beads for this abacus shows us the size of the number. This number has 2 hundreds, 3 tens and 1 unit. It is 231.

able

When you can do something, you are **able** to do it.
I am able to read this book now.

about

1 **About** means to do with.
My book is about Africa.
2 **About** also means not exactly.
I'll be home at about 6 o'clock.

accident   accidents

An **accident** is something which happens that was not planned.
The car slid on the ice, causing an accident.
Mum broke the cup by accident.

ache   aches

An **ache** is a pain that goes on hurting, like toothache.
I have had an ache in my leg all day.

acorn   acorns

An **acorn** is a small nut that grows on an oak tree. Oak trees grow from **acorns**.

act   acts, acting, acted

1 You **act** when you do something.
The doctor acted quickly to save his life.
2 When you pretend to be someone in a play or film, you are **acting**.

active

An **active** person is full of life and is doing something.

actor   actors

An **actor** is a man or woman who acts in a play or a film.

actress   actresses

A female actor is sometimes called an **actress**.

add   adds, adding, added

1 If you **add** one thing to another, you put it with something else.
2 If you **add** numbers, you find out how many they make altogether. The symbol + means **add**.
One add one makes two. 1 + 1 = 2

addition

Addition is what you do when you add numbers or other things together.

address addresses
Your **address** is where you live.
My address is 15 Castle Street, Dover.

adjective adjectives
An **adjective** is a word that
describes a person or thing.

The little girl lived in an old house.
adjectives

adult adults
An **adult** is a grown-up person.

adventure adventures
You have an **adventure** when
something exciting happens to you.

adverb adverbs
An **adverb** is a word that tells you
more about a verb.

The wind blew wildly.
adverb

aeroplane aeroplanes
An **aeroplane** is a flying machine
that carries people and things.

afraid
When you are **afraid**, you are
scared or frightened.

after
Something that is **after** something
else is later than it.
I watch television after school.

afternoon afternoons
The **afternoon** is the part of the day
between 12 noon and evening.

again
If you do something **again**, you do it
once more.
*Sarah rang the bell and then she rang
it again.*

against
1 If you put a ladder **against** a wall,
you put it so close that it touches the
wall.
2 If you are playing **against** a team,
you are on the other side.

age ages
Your **age** is the number of years you
have lived.

ago
Ago means in the past.
Joe started school two years ago.

agree **agrees, agreeing, agreed**
When you **agree** with someone, you think the same as they do.
*The girls **agreed** to go swimming.*

air
Air is made of gases. It is all around but you cannot see it. People must breathe **air** to live.

airport **airports**
Aeroplanes land and take off at an **airport**.

alien **aliens**
An **alien** is a creature from another planet.
*The **aliens** arrived in a spaceship.*

alike
People or things that are nearly the same are **alike**.
*Arun and Ram look **alike** because they are brothers.*

alive
When people, animals and plants are living, they are **alive**.

all
1 All means each member or part.
All my family came to the wedding.
2 All also means the whole of something.
*Liz ate **all** the jelly.*

alligator **alligators**
An **alligator** is a scaly reptile that looks like a crocodile. It lives on land and in water.

alliteration
Using words which begin with the same sound closely together is called **alliteration**.
*"Green grass" is an example of **alliteration**.*

allow **allows, allowing, allowed**
When you **allow** someone to do something, you let them do it.
*Kate **allowed** Peter to use her ruler.*

almost
Almost means nearly but not quite.
*It was **almost** 3 o'clock.*

alone
You are **alone** if there is nobody with you.

aloud
When you read **aloud**, people can hear you.

alphabet **alphabets**
An **alphabet** is all the letters used in writing, set out in a special order.
There is an **alphabet** down the side of this page.

alphabetical

Alphabetical means in the same order as the letters of the alphabet.

The words in this dictionary are listed in **alphabetical** *order.*

already

Already means before now.

I have **already** *had my dinner.*

also

Also means as well.

I can swim and dive. I can **also** *skate.*

altogether

When you add things up, the answer is what you have **altogether**.

Rasheed has four stickers and Anna has five, so they have nine stickers **altogether**.

always

If something **always** happens, it happens every time.

This bus is **always** *late.*

amazing

If something is **amazing**, you are filled with a feeling of great surprise.

ambulance **ambulances**

An **ambulance** is a special van that takes sick people to hospital.

amount **amounts**

The **amount** of something is how much of it there is.

There was a huge **amount** *of snow on the road.*

amphibian **amphibians**

An **amphibian** is an animal that lives part of its life in water and part on the land. A frog is an **amphibian**.

analogue

The face of an **analogue** clock or watch has numbers from 1 to 12. Two hands point to the numbers to tell you the time.

ancient

Ancient means very old or long ago.

The Pyramids were built in **ancient** *times.*

angry **angrier, angriest**

If you are very annoyed and upset, you feel **angry**.

animal **animals**

An **animal** is a living creature that is not a plant. For example, dogs, birds, fish, insects and people are **animals**.

ankle **ankles**

Your **ankle** is the part of your leg that joins your foot. (See page 174.)

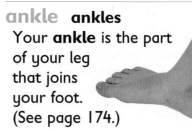

Aa

b
c
d
e
f
g
h
i
j
k
l
m
n
o
p
q
r
s
t
u
v
w
x
y
z

anniversary anniversaries
An **anniversary** is a date you remember each year because something special happened on it.
The 25th of May is my grandparents' wedding anniversary.

announce announces, announcing, announced
When you **announce** something, you say it aloud to let everyone know.
Miss Jones announced the winner.

annoy annoys, annoying, annoyed
If you **annoy** someone, you make them angry.

another
1 Another means one more.
Can I have another cake?
2 Another can also mean different.
Try to do the sum another way.

answer answers, answering, answered
1 If you **answer**, you speak to someone who has just spoken to you.
2 You give an **answer** when somebody asks you a question.

ant ants
An **ant** is a tiny insect. **Ants** live in large groups.

antelope antelopes
An **antelope** is a wild animal from Africa that looks like a deer. It can run very fast.

anticlockwise
If you go **anticlockwise**, you move in the opposite direction to the hands of a clock.

antonym antonyms
An **antonym** is a word that means the opposite of another word. Hot is the **antonym** of cold. Fast is an **antonym** of slow. (See page 181.)

anxious
If you are **anxious**, you are worried about something.

any
1 Any means one, some or a few.
Have you got any crisps?
2 Any also means whichever you want.
I'm not busy, so you can come any day.

anybody
Anybody means any person.

anyone
Anyone is another word for anybody.

anything
Anything means any thing at all.

anywhere
Anywhere means in any place at all.
I'll meet you anywhere you like.

apart

If something falls **apart**, it falls to pieces.

ape apes

An **ape** is a monkey without a tail. Gorillas and chimpanzees are **apes**.

apologize or apologise
apologizes, apologizing, apologized

If you **apologize**, you say you are sorry for something you have done.
Sue apologized for being late.

appear appears, appearing, appeared

When something **appears**, you can suddenly see it.

apple apples

An **apple** is a round, juicy fruit that grows on a tree. Its skin can be red, green or yellow.

April

April is the fourth month of the year. It has 30 days.

apron aprons

You wear an **apron** over your clothes to stop them getting dirty when you paint or cook.

arch arches

An **arch** is part of a building or bridge. It has a curved top and straight sides.

area areas

An **area** is a part of a country or place.
This park has a special area for dogs.

argue argues, arguing, argued

If you **argue** with someone, you quarrel with them.

argument arguments

An **argument** happens when people argue.

arm arms

Your **arm** is a part of your body. It is between your hand and your shoulder. (See page 174.)

armour

Armour is metal clothing or plates worn to protect the body.
Long ago, soldiers wore suits of armour.

army **armies**
An **army** is a large group of soldiers trained to fight on land.

arrange **arranges, arranging, arranged**
1 If you **arrange** to do something, you make plans to do it.
*Mum and Dad **arranged** a trip to France.*
2 If you **arrange** things, you put them in order.
*Lisa **arranged** the books in neat piles.*

array **arrays**
An **array** is a group of things set out neatly in columns and rows.

arrive **arrives, arriving, arrived**
When you **arrive** at a place, you get there.

arrow **arrows**
1 An **arrow** is a thin stick with a point at one end and feathers at the other. It is shot from a bow.
2 An **arrow** is also a sign that points to something or shows you the way.

art
Art is paintings, drawings and sculptures.
*I saw lots of pictures at the **art** show.*

ask **asks, asking, asked**
1 You **ask** someone a question when you want to find the answer.
*"When is the party?" Simon **asked**.*
2 You **ask** for something when you want to be given it.
*"May I have some pudding?" Amy **asked**.*

asleep
When you are **asleep** your eyes are closed. You do not know what is happening around you.

assembly **assemblies**
An **assembly** is a group of people meeting together.
*We have school **assembly** every day.*

assistant **assistants**
An **assistant** is someone who helps another person.

astronaut **astronauts**
An **astronaut** flies in a spacecraft and travels in space.

ate See **eat**.

atlas **atlases**
An **atlas** is a book of maps.

attack **attacks, attacking, attacked**
If you **attack** someone, you try to harm them.

attention
When you watch and listen carefully, you are paying **attention**.

attract **attracts, attracting, attracted**
If something **attracts** you, you become interested in it.

audience **audiences**
The people who watch or listen to a concert, film or TV show are the **audience**.
*The **audience** laughed at the clowns.*

August
August is the eighth month of the year. It has 31 days.

aunt or **auntie**
aunts or **aunties**
Your **aunt** is the sister of your mother or father, or the wife of your uncle.

author **authors**
An **author** is a person who writes books or plays.

automatic
An **automatic** machine does things on its own.
*An **automatic** washing machine washes clothes on its own.*

autumn
Autumn is the season between summer and winter. It gets cooler and the leaves fall off many trees.

awake
When you are **awake**, your eyes are open. You know what is happening around you.

away
If you go **away**, you leave the place where you are.

awful
Awful means very bad.
*Dad had an **awful** cold.*

axe **axes**
An **axe** is a tool with a handle and a sharp metal edge. People chop wood with an **axe**.

a

Bb

c
d
e
f
g
h
i
j
k
l
m
n
o
p
q
r
s
t
u
v
w
x
y
z

baby babies
A **baby** is a very young child.

back backs
1 The **back** of something is the opposite side to the front.
2 Your **back** is the part of the body between your neck and your bottom.

backwards
1 If you walk **backwards**, you are walking in the direction that is behind you.
2 **Backwards** is the opposite way to forwards. If you say the alphabet **backwards**, you start at Z and finish at A.

bacon
Bacon is a kind of meat. It comes from a pig.
*We had eggs and **bacon** for breakfast.*

bad worse, worst
1 Something **bad** is not good.
2 Food is **bad** when it is too old to eat.

badge badges
A **badge** is a small sign with words and pictures. You wear it on your clothes.

badger badgers
A **badger** is a wild animal. It has black and white fur and lives underground. It comes out at night to hunt for food.

bag bags
A **bag** is used to hold things. It can be made of cloth, plastic, paper or leather.

bake bakes, baking, baked
When you **bake** food, you cook it in an oven.

baker bakers
A **baker** bakes and sells bread and cakes.

balance balances, balancing, balanced
1 When you **balance** something, you keep it steady and stop it from falling.
2 A **balance** is a weighing machine.
*Put these two parcels on the **balance** to see which one is heavier.*

ball   balls

A **ball** is a round object. You can throw, catch, hit, roll or kick it.

ballet

Ballet is a special kind of dancing. It often tells a story.

balloon   balloons

A **balloon** is a thin rubber bag. It can be blown up to make it float in the air.

banana   bananas

A **banana** is a long fruit. You peel off its thick yellow skin to eat it.

band   bands

1 A **band** is a group of people who play music together.
2 A **band** is also a narrow strip of something, such as a rubber band.

bandage   bandages

A **bandage** is a strip of material. It is put over a cut to keep it clean.

bang   bangs, banging, banged

1 A **bang** is a sudden loud noise.
The balloon burst with a bang.
2 When you **bang** something, you hit or shut it noisily.
Harry banged the door shut.

bank   banks

1 People put their money in a **bank** to keep it safe.
2 A **bank** is also the land near the side of a river.

bar   bars

1 A **bar** is a long piece of wood or metal.
2 A **bar** is also something made in a rectangular shape, like a **bar** of soap or a **bar** of chocolate.

bare

1 **Bare** means uncovered.
Kim took her shoes off and danced in her bare feet.
2 **Bare** can also mean empty.
The fridge was bare so Mum bought some more food.

bargain   bargains

A **bargain** is something that is worth more than you pay for it.

bark   barks, barking, barked

1 The **bark** of a tree is the hard part that covers its trunk.
2 A dog that **barks** makes a short, loud sound.

barn   barns

A **barn** is a large building on a farm. Farmers store their crops in **barns**.

base

The **base** is the bottom part of something.
The boys camped at the base of the mountain.

a

Bb

c
d
e
f
g
h
i
j
k
l
m
n
o
p
q
r
s
t
u
v
w
x
y
z

basket baskets
A **basket** is a container made of thin strips. It is used to store or carry things.

bat bats
1 A **bat** is a piece of wood with a handle. It is used to hit a ball.
2 A **bat** is also an animal. It looks like a mouse with wings. **Bats** fly at night and hang upside down when they sleep.

bath baths
A **bath** is a long container. You fill it with water and sit in it to wash your body.

bathroom bathrooms
A **bathroom** is the room where you wash yourself.

battery batteries
A **battery** is a small object that gives electricity. Watches and torches need the energy from **batteries** to work.

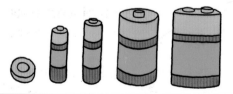

battle battles
A **battle** is a fight between armies.

beach beaches
A **beach** is the land at the edge of the sea. It is covered in sand or pebbles.

beak beaks
A bird's **beak** is the hard part of its mouth.

bean beans
A **bean** is a vegetable. There are different kinds, like red kidney **beans** and runner **beans**.

bear bears
A **bear** is a large, wild furry animal with claws. Grizzly **bears** and polar **bears** are very big and heavy.

beard beards
A **beard** is the hair that grows on a man's chin and cheeks.

beat beats, beating, beat, beaten
1 When you **beat** someone in a race, you finish before they do.
2 If you **beat** something, you hit it again and again.
*The soldier was **beating** the drum.*

beautiful
Something that is lovely to see or hear is **beautiful**.
*The sunset was **beautiful** tonight.*

because

Because is a word used to give a reason why.

We were late because we missed the bus.

bed **beds**

A **bed** is a piece of furniture you sleep on.

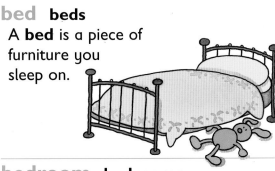

bedroom **bedrooms**

A **bedroom** is the room where you sleep. A **bedroom** has a bed in it.

bedtime

Bedtime is the time of day when you usually go to bed.

bee **bees**

A **bee** is an insect with wings. **Bees** make honey. Some **bees** live in beehives.

beetle **beetles**

A **beetle** is an insect. It has hard shiny wings.

before

If something is **before** something else, it happens earlier than it.

I clean my teeth before I go to bed.

begin **begins, beginning, began, begun**

You **begin** something when you start to do it.

I always begin to get hungry at playtime.

behave **behaves, behaving, behaved**

When you **behave** yourself, you are being good.

behind

If you are **behind** something, you are at the back of it.

Lucy hid behind the fence.

believe **believes, believing, believed**

When you **believe** something, you think it is true.

bell **bells**

A **bell** is something that rings when you hit, shake or press it.

The school bell rings every morning.

belong **belongs, belonging, belonged**

When something **belongs** to you, you own it.

This bag belongs to me. It has my name on it.

belt **belts**

A **belt** is a long strip of leather or cloth. It is worn around the waist.

bend **bends, bending, bent**

1 If you **bend** something, it is no longer straight.

2 A **bend** in a road is where it goes round a corner.

a

Bb

c
d
e
f
g
h
i
j
k
l
m
n
o
p
q
r
s
t
u
v
w
x
y
z

berry berries
A **berry** is a small, juicy fruit that grows on bushes or trees.

best
If you are the **best**, you are better than anyone else at something.
Pete was the best footballer ever.
See **good** and **well**.

better
1 If you do something **better** than someone, they are not as good at it as you are.
John is good at drawing, but Roberto is even better.
2 If you have been ill, you are **better** when you feel well again.
See **good** and **well**.

between
1 Something that is **between** two other things is in the middle.
The number 22 is between numbers 21 and 23.
2 If you share something equally **between** two people, you give them the same amount or number.
Jenny and Leela shared six sweets equally between them. They got three each.

bicycle bicycles
A **bicycle** is a vehicle with two wheels. You sit on it and turn the pedals with your feet.

big bigger, biggest
Big means large in size.
This is too big for me now. It will fit me when I'm bigger.

bike bikes
Bike is another word for bicycle.

bin bins
A **bin** is a container. You put bread in a bread **bin** and rubbish in a rubbish **bin**.

bird birds
A **bird** is an animal with feathers. It has two wings and two legs. Most **birds** can fly.

birthday birthdays
Your **birthday** is the day you were born on.
My birthday is on the first day of August.

biscuit biscuits
A **biscuit** is a kind of thin, hard cake.

bit bits
1 *Sam bit the apple.*
See **bite**.
2 A **bit** is a very small piece of something.
The cup smashed into bits.

bite bites, biting, bit, bitten

When you **bite** something, you use your teeth to cut or tear it.
Sam is biting an apple.

blackberry blackberries

A **blackberry** is a small black fruit that grows on a bush.

blackbird blackbirds

A **blackbird** is a common bird. The male **blackbird** has black feathers and a yellow beak. The female is brown.

blackboard blackboards

A **blackboard** is used in a classroom. The teacher writes on it with chalk.

blade blades

A **blade** is the sharp part of a knife or an axe.

blame blames, blaming, blamed

1 If you **blame** someone, you say that they have done something wrong.
2 If you take the **blame**, you say that something was your fault.

blanket blankets

A **blanket** is a piece of thick cloth. It keeps you warm in bed.

blew See blow.

blind blinds

1 A **blind** person cannot see.
2 You pull a **blind** down over a window to keep out the light.

block blocks

A **block** is a solid piece of something.
Lizzie built a tower of wooden blocks.

block graph block graphs

A **block graph** is a kind of graph. The information is shown using blocks arranged in columns.

What we like to drink

number of children

juice milk tea water cola

blood

Blood is the red liquid that goes around inside your body.

blouse blouses

A **blouse** is a kind of shirt worn by girls and women. (See page 176.)

blow blows, blowing, blew, blown

1 You **blow** when you send air out through your mouth and nose.
Dad is blowing up the balloons for my party.

2 When the wind **blows**, the air moves faster.

a

Bb

c
d
e
f
g
h
i
j
k
l
m
n
o
p
q
r
s
t
u
v
w
x
y
z

a

Bb

c

d

e

f

g

h

i

j

k

l

m

n

o

p

q

r

s

t

u

v

w

x

y

z

blunt **blunter, bluntest**
When something is **blunt**, it is not sharp.

blurb
The **blurb** is the information about a book on its back cover.

boat **boats**
A **boat** is a vehicle that travels across water.

body **bodies**
A person's **body** is the whole of them.
*Your skin covers all your **body**.*

boil **boils, boiling, boiled**
1 Water **boils** when it gets very hot. You can see bubbles and steam.
2 When you **boil** food, you cook it in **boiling** water.

bold **bolder, boldest**
1 A **bold** person is brave. They are not afraid to do dangerous things.
2 Bold letters are dark and heavy, like the word **bold** in this sentence.

bomb **bombs**
A **bomb** is a weapon. It blows things apart.

bone **bones**
Bones are the hard white parts inside your body. They all join together to make your skeleton.

bonfire **bonfires**
A **bonfire** is a large fire that is lit outside.

bonnet **bonnets**
1 The **bonnet** is part of a car. (See page 175.)
2 A **bonnet** is a kind of hat.

book **books**
A **book** has pages held together inside a cover. The pages show words or pictures.

boot **boots**
1 A **boot** is a kind of shoe. It covers your foot and part of your leg.
2 A **boot** is also part of a car. (See page 175.)

bored
When you are **bored,** you are not interested in what you are doing.
*Adam was **bored** because it was raining and there was nothing to do.*

boring
Something **boring** is dull and not interesting.

born
A baby is **born** when it comes out of its mother's body.

borrow **borrows, borrowing, borrowed**
When you **borrow** something, you use it and give it back.
*Anil **borrows** books from the library.*

both

Both means two, not just one.
Keep both hands on the handlebars!

bottle   **bottles**

A **bottle** is a container for liquids.
It is made of glass
or plastic and is
narrow at the top.
*Dad bought two
bottles of cola
for the party.*

bottom   **bottoms**

1 The lowest part of something is its
bottom.
*The ball rolled down to the bottom of
the hill.*
2 Your **bottom** is the part of your
body that you sit on.

bought   See **buy**.

bounce   **bounces, bouncing,
bounced**
When something
bounces, it jumps
back from a
hard surface.

bow   **bows, bowing, bowed**

1 *(sounds like* **cow***)*
When you **bow**, you
bend over at the waist.
Jess bowed to the audience.

2 *(sounds like* **no***)*
A **bow** is a kind of knot.

3 *(sounds like* **no***)*
A **bow** is also a bent piece
of wood used for shooting arrows.

bowl   **bowls**

A **bowl** is a deep dish. You can put
soup or breakfast cereal in a **bowl**.

box   **boxes**

A **box** is a container with straight
sides. It sometimes has a lid.
Liam's shoes came in a cardboard box.

boy   **boys**

A **boy** is a child who will be a man
when he grows up.

bracelet   **bracelets**

A **bracelet** is a piece of jewellery
that you wear around your wrist.

brain   **brains**

Your **brain** is inside your head and
controls your body. You think and
remember with your **brain**.

brake   **brakes**

The **brakes** of a bicycle or car make
it slow down or stop. (See page 175.)

branch   **branches**

The **branches** of
a tree grow out
from the trunk.

brave   **braver, bravest**

A **brave** person faces danger or pain
without showing fear.

bread

Bread is a food. It is made from flour
and baked in an oven.
Nick likes bread and peanut butter.

a
Bb
c
d
e
f
g
h
i
j
k
l
m
n
o
p
q
r
s
t
u
v
w
x
y
z

break breaks, breaking, broke, broken

1 When something **breaks**, it falls into pieces.
When Mum dropped the plate, it broke into little pieces.

2 When a machine is **broken**, it does not work properly.
The TV is broken. I can't watch cartoons.

breakfast
Breakfast is the first meal of the day.

breathe breathes, breathing, breathed
When you **breathe**, you take air in through your mouth and nose and then let it out again.

brick bricks
A **brick** is a block made from clay.
Bricks are used to build houses.

bride brides
A **bride** is a woman on her wedding day.

bridesmaid   bride   bridegroom

bridegroom bridegrooms
A **bridegroom** is a man on his wedding day.

bridesmaid bridesmaids
A **bridesmaid** is a girl who helps a bride on her wedding day.

bridge bridges
A **bridge** is built over a road, river or railway line so that people and vehicles can cross it.

bright brighter, brightest
Something **bright** shines strongly.

brilliant
1 A **brilliant** light or colour is very bright.
2 A **brilliant** person is very clever.
3 A **brilliant** film or book is very, very good.

bring brings, bringing, brought
If you **bring** someone or something to a place, you take them with you.
Molly is bringing her sister to my house.

broke See **break**.

broken See **break**.

broom brooms
A **broom** is a brush with a long handle. It is used for sweeping floors.

brother brothers
Your **brother** is a boy who has the same parents as you do.

brought See **bring**.

brush **brushes**
A **brush** has a handle with lots of stiff hairs joined to it. **Brushes** come in lots of shapes and sizes. You use a **hairbrush** to make your hair tidy. You use a **toothbrush** to clean your teeth. **Paintbrushes** are for painting.

bubble **bubbles**
1 A **bubble** is a ball of air. It is surrounded by a thin layer of liquid.
Look at Zina's lovely bubbles! She is using a soapy liquid.

2 In a cartoon, what people say is written in **speech bubbles**.

bucket **buckets**
A **bucket** is a container with a handle. It is made from plastic or metal.
Mai Ling filled her bucket with sand.

bud **buds**
A **bud** is a young flower or leaf before it opens.
In the spring, buds appear on the trees.

build **builds, building, built**
You **build** something when you put all its different parts together.

building **buildings**
A **building** has walls and a roof. Houses and schools are **buildings**. See **build**.

built See **build**.

bulb **bulbs**
1 The **bulb** of a plant like an onion or tulip is the round part that grows in the soil.
2 A **bulb** is also the glass part of an electric lamp. It gives out light.

bull **bulls**
Cows and **bulls** are large farm animals. A **bull** is the male animal.

bullet **bullets**
A **bullet** is a small piece of metal. It is fired from a gun.

bump **bumps, bumping, bumped**
1 If you **bump** into something, you knock into it suddenly.
Charlie bumped into the table and knocked over the lamp.
2 A **bump** is a swelling or lump on your body.
Rose had a bump on her head.

bumper **bumpers**
A **bumper** is part of a car. (See page 175.)

bunch **bunches**
A **bunch** is a group of things that are joined or held together.
I gave my mum a bunch of flowers. Dad bought her a bunch of grapes.

a
Bb
c
d
e
f
g
h
i
j
k
l
m
n
o
p
q
r
s
t
u
v
w
x
y
z

a

Bb

c d e f g h i j k l m n o p q r s t u v w x y z

bungalow bungalows
A **bungalow** is a house with no upstairs.

burger burgers
A **burger** is a flat, round piece of cooked meat in a bun.

burglar burglars
A **burglar** goes into a building to steal things.

buried See **bury**.

burn burns, burning, burned, burnt
1 If something **burns**, it is on fire.
2 When you **burn** something, you hurt it or damage it by fire or heat.
3 A **burn** is a mark or injury caused by fire or heat.

burst bursts, bursting, burst
1 When something **bursts**, it breaks suddenly.
*The balloon **burst** with a loud bang.*
2 When somebody **bursts** into something, they do it suddenly.
*The baby **burst** into tears.*

bury buries, burying, buried
If you **bury** something, you put it in a hole in the ground and cover it up.
*The dog **buried** the bone in the garden.*

bus buses
A **bus** is a large vehicle with lots of seats. It carries people from one place to another.

bush bushes
A **bush** is a large woody plant with lots of branches.

bus stop bus stops
Buses stop at a **bus stop** to let people get on or off.

busy busier, busiest
A **busy** person has a lot to do.

butcher butchers
A **butcher** cuts up meat and sells it.

butter
Butter is a yellow food made from milk. You spread it on bread.

butterfly butterflies
A **butterfly** is an insect. It has large white or coloured wings.

button buttons
A **button** is a small round object sewn onto your clothes. You push it through a buttonhole to do your clothes up.

buy buys, buying, bought
You **buy** something when you pay money to get it.
*I **bought** this book with my birthday money.*

buzz buzzes, buzzing, buzzed
If something **buzzes**, it makes a humming sound like a bee.

Cc

cabbage cabbages

A **cabbage** is a vegetable with green or purple leaves.

cable cables

1 A **cable** is a bundle of wires covered in rubber which carries electricity.
2 Cable television reaches people's homes through underground wires.

café cafés

You go to a **café** to have a snack or a drink.

cage cages

A **cage** is a box or room with bars. Birds and animals are sometimes kept in **cages**.

cake cakes

Cake is a sweet food. It is made by baking a mixture of flour, eggs, sugar and fat.

calculate calculates, calculating, calculated

If you **calculate** something, you work it out.
Calculate the answer to 8 + 3 + 4.

calculation calculations

A **calculation** is what you do when you work something out in maths.
*Can you do this **calculation** in your head?*

calculator calculators

A **calculator** is a small machine for doing calculations.

calendar calendars

A **calendar** is a list that shows the days, weeks and months of the year.
*I marked my birthday on the **calendar**.*

calf calves

1 A **calf** is a young cow or bull.
2 Your **calf** is also the back of your leg, between your knee and your heel. (See page 174.)

call calls, calling, called

1 If you **call** a person something, you give them a name.
2 If you **call** someone or give them a **call**, you telephone them.
3 If you **call** out, you speak loudly, sometimes with pain or excitement.
4 If you **call** on someone, you go to see them.

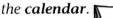

a
b
Cc
d
e
f
g
h
i
j
k
l
m
n
o
p
q
r
s
t
u
v
w
x
y
z

calves See **calf**.

came See **come**.

camel **camels**
A **camel** is an animal that has one or two large humps on its back. **Camels** live in deserts and can travel a long way without water.

camera **cameras**
A **camera** is a machine that takes photographs, or film or television pictures.

camp **camps, camping, camped**
1 A **camp** is a group of tents or huts where people live or stay.
2 When you go **camping**, you live in a tent for a short time.

can **could; cans**
1 If you **can** do something, you are able to do it.
Peter can touch his toes.
2 A **can** is a metal container for liquids and food.
Mum opened a can of beans.

canal **canals**
A **canal** is a strip of water for boats to travel on. **Canals** are made by people.

candle **candles**
A **candle** is a stick of wax with string through the middle. You burn a **candle** to give you light.

cannot
If you **cannot** do something, you are not able to do it.
Paul cannot touch his toes.

can't
Can't is short for cannot.

cap **caps**
A **cap** is a small hat. It has a stiff piece sticking out at the front.

capacity
The **capacity** of something is the amount that it can hold.

capital **capitals**
1 A **capital** letter is a letter used at the beginning of a sentence or a name. **Capital** letters are sometimes called upper-case letters.
A B C D are capital letters and a b c d are lower-case letters.
2 A country's **capital** is the city from which it is controlled.
The capital of Italy is Rome.

captain **captains**
1 The leader of a group or team is often called the **captain**.
Rosie was captain of the rounders team.
2 A **captain** is also the person in charge of a ship or an aeroplane.

caption **captions**
A **caption** is the writing under a picture.

car cars

A **car** is a vehicle with four wheels and an engine. It can carry four or five people. (See page 175.)

caravan caravans

A **caravan** is a small house on wheels. It is pulled by a car or lorry.

card cards

1 A **card** is a piece of stiff paper with pictures and words on it. You send **cards** to people at special times like birthdays or when they are ill.
2 Playing **cards** have pictures or numbers on them. They are used to play games.

cardboard

Cardboard is very thick, stiff paper. It is used for making boxes.

care cares, caring, cared

1 If you **care** about something, it is important to you.
2 If you **care** for something, you look after it.
*It's Peshpa's turn to **care** for the hamster.*

careful

When you are **careful**, you think about what you are doing. You try not to make mistakes.

careless

When you are **careless**, you do not think about what you are doing. You often make mistakes.

carpet carpets

A **carpet** covers floors and stairs. It is usually made from wool.

carriage carriages

1 A **carriage** is a vehicle that carries people. It is pulled by horses.

2 A **carriage** is also the part of a train where passengers sit.

carrot carrots

A **carrot** is a long, orange vegetable. It grows under the ground.

carry carries, carrying, carried

If you **carry** something, you hold it and take it somewhere.

cartoon cartoons

1 In a **cartoon** film, all the pictures are drawn.
2 A **cartoon** is also a drawing that makes you laugh.

case cases

A **case** is a container to carry or keep things in.
*I packed my **case** with clothes for my holiday.*

a
b
Cc
d
e
f
g
h
i
j
k
l
m
n
o
p
q
r
s
t
u
v
w
x
y
z

a
b
Cc
d
e
f
g
h
i
j
k
l
m
n
o
p
q
r
s
t
u
v
w
x
y
z

castle **castles**
A **castle** is an old stone building. It has thick, high walls to protect the people inside.

cat **cats**
A **cat** is an animal with soft fur and sharp claws. Small **cats** are kept as pets. Lions and tigers are large **cats** that live in the wild.

catch **catches, catching, caught**
1 If you **catch** something that is moving, you stop it and hold it.
2 If you **catch** an illness, you become ill with it.
3 When you **catch** a bus, you get on it.

caterpillar **caterpillars**
A **caterpillar** is a creature that looks like a worm with legs. It becomes a butterfly or a moth.

cattle
Cows and bulls kept on a farm are **cattle**. Meat called beef and milk come from **cattle**.

caught See **catch**.

cauliflower **cauliflowers**
A **cauliflower** is a vegetable. It has a hard white centre and green leaves around the outside.

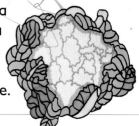

cave **caves**
A **cave** is a hollow place in the side of a mountain or underground.

CD **CDs**
A **CD** or compact disc is a flat plastic disc. It stores music, or information for use by a computer.

ceiling **ceilings**
A **ceiling** is the flat surface that covers the top of a room.

centimetre **centimetres**
Length, height, width or distance are measured in **centimetres**. There are 100 **centimetres** (cm) in a metre.

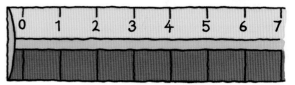

centre **centres**
1 The **centre** is the middle point of anything.
2 A **centre** is a place where people go for a special reason, like a health **centre**.

century **centuries**
A **century** is one hundred years.

cereal **cereals**
Breakfast **cereals** are foods eaten with milk. They are made from the seeds of oats, wheat or corn.

chain **chains**
A **chain** is a row of rings joined together in a line. **Chains** are usually made of metal.

chair **chairs**
A **chair** is a seat for one person. It has a back and sometimes has arms.

chalk
Chalk is a kind of soft white rock. Sticks of **chalk** are used for writing on a blackboard.

champion **champions**
A **champion** is someone who has won a competition.
*At the Olympics, the **champions** win gold medals.*

change **changes, changing, changed**
1 If you **change** something, you make it different.
2 When you get **changed**, you put on different clothes.
3 If you give too much money to pay for something, you are given **change**.
*I gave the shopkeeper too much money so he gave me some **change**.*

channel **channels**
1 A **channel** is a radio or television station.
*I switched over to **Channel** 2.*
2 A **channel** is also a narrow stretch of water.

chapter **chapters**
A **chapter** is a part of a book.
*Open your books at **Chapter** 3.*

character **characters**
A **character** is a person in a story, play or film.

charge **charges, charging, charged**
1 If someone **charges** you for something, they ask you to pay for it.
2 If you **charge**, you run forward, often to attack someone.
*The angry elephant **charged** through the forest.*
3 The person in **charge** of something is in control of it.
*Miss Dent is in **charge** of the class.*

chase **chases, chasing, chased**
If you **chase** someone, you run after them.

cheap **cheaper, cheapest**
Something **cheap** does not cost very much.

check **checks, checking, checked**
If you **check** something, you look at it carefully to see if it is all right.

checkout **checkouts**
A **checkout** is the place in a supermarket where you pay for your shopping.

cheek **cheeks**
Your **cheeks** are the soft parts on both sides of your face.
(See page 174.)

a
b
Cc
d
e
f
g
h
i
j
k
l
m
n
o
p
q
r
s
t
u
v
w
x
y
z

29

a
b
Cc
d
e
f
g
h
i
j
k
l
m
n
o
p
q
r
s
t
u
v
w
x
y
z

cheese cheeses
Cheese is a hard or soft food made from milk.

chemist chemists
A **chemist** is a person who sells medicines.

cherry cherries
A **cherry** is a small round fruit with a stone in the middle. **Cherries** can be red, yellow or black.

chest chests
1 Your **chest** is the front part of your body between your neck and your tummy. (See page 174.)
2 A **chest** is a strong box with a lid.

chew chews, chewing, chewed
When you **chew** something, you keep biting it with your teeth to break it up.
Chew your food well before you swallow it.

chick chicks
A **chick** is a baby bird.

chicken chickens
A **chicken** is a large bird kept by farmers. **Chickens** give us eggs and meat.

chickenpox
Chickenpox is an illness. You get a fever and red spots on your skin.

chief chiefs
A **chief** is the leader of a group of people.

child children
A **child** is a young boy or girl.
*The **children** are playing on the swings.*

chimney chimneys
A **chimney** is an opening in a roof above a fire. Smoke goes up through the **chimney** into the air.

chimpanzee chimpanzees
A **chimpanzee** is a type of African ape. **Chimpanzees** are smaller than gorillas.

chin chins
Your **chin** is the bottom part of your face, below your mouth. (See page 174.)

chip chips
1 A **chip** is a long piece of potato fried in oil.
2 If a cup has a **chip** in it, there is a small piece missing.
3 A **chip** is also a very small piece of metal that makes a computer work.

chocolate chocolates
Chocolate is a sweet, brown food that often comes in a bar. Drinks, cakes and puddings can taste of **chocolate**, too.

choose chooses, choosing, chose, chosen
If you **choose** something, you decide which one you want.
*I've **chosen** the biggest cake!*

chop chops, chopping, chopped
When you **chop** something, you cut it with a knife or axe.

chose See **choose**.

chosen See **choose**.

Christmas
Christmas is the 25th of December, when people celebrate Jesus Christ's birth. People often decorate a **Christmas** tree and give each other presents.

church churches
A **church** is a building where some people go to pray.

cinema cinemas
A **cinema** is a building where films are shown.

circle circles
A **circle** is a perfect round flat shape. The letter O is a **circle**.

circular
Anything in the shape of a circle is **circular**.

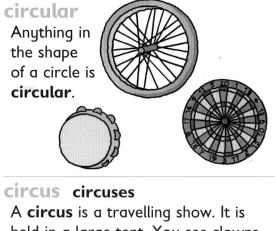

circus circuses
A **circus** is a travelling show. It is held in a large tent. You see clowns at a **circus**.

city cities
A **city** is a very large place where lots of people live. **Cities** are bigger than towns.

clap claps, clapping, clapped
When you **clap**, you make a noise by hitting your hands together.
*The children **clapped** to show they enjoyed Ravi's story.*

class classes
A **class** is a group of people who learn together.

classroom classrooms
A class has its lessons in a **classroom**.

claw claws
A **claw** is the sharp curved nail of an animal.
*The cat dug its **claws** into the sofa.*

a
b
Cc
d
e
f
g
h
i
j
k
l
m
n
o
p
q
r
s
t
u
v
w
x
y
z

a
b
Cc
d
e
f
g
h
i
j
k
l
m
n
o
p
q
r
s
t
u
v
w
x
y
z

clay
Clay is a kind of earth that is used to make bricks and pots.

clean cleans, cleaning, cleaned; cleaner, cleanest
1 You **clean** something to get the dirt off it.
2 Something that is **clean** has no dirty marks on it.

clear clearer, clearest
1 Something **clear** is easy to see through, like glass.
2 When something is **clear**, it is easy to see, hear or understand.
*This book has nice **clear** pictures.*
3 If something is **clear**, nothing covers it or gets in the way.
*The road was **clear** of snow.*

clever cleverer, cleverest
A **clever** person can do things easily and quickly.

cliff cliffs
A **cliff** is a hill with a steep side that goes straight down. **Cliffs** are usually near the sea.

climb climbs, climbing, climbed
You **climb** when you go up or down something high.
*My sister Lin **climbed** to the very top of the tree.*

clinic clinics
People go to a **clinic** for help when they are not well.
Ben's eye hurt, so he went to the eye clinic.

cloak cloaks
A **cloak** is a coat that has no sleeves.

clock clocks
A **clock** is a machine that tells you the time.

clockwise
If you go **clockwise**, you move in the same direction as the hands of a clock.

close closes, closing, closed; closer, closest
1 (*sounds like* **nose**) When you **close** something, you shut it.
2 (*sounds like* **dose**) **Close** means near.

closed
Closed means shut.

cloth cloths
1 **Cloth** is a soft material like cotton or wool. Your clothes are made of **cloth**.
2 A **cloth** is used to clean or cover things.

clothes

You wear **clothes** to keep you warm and dry. Jumpers and trousers are **clothes**. (See pages 176–177.)
When I get up, I put on my school clothes.

cloud   clouds

You can see white or grey **clouds** floating in the sky. **Clouds** are made of very small drops of water which sometimes fall as rain.

clown   clowns

A **clown** does silly things to make people laugh. **Clowns** have painted faces and wear funny clothes.

club   clubs

A **club** is a group of people who meet often to do the same thing.
Jane and Tom go to the swimming club every Friday.

clue   clues

A **clue** helps you to solve a problem or a mystery.

coach   coaches

1 A **coach** is a bus used for long journeys.
2 A **coach** is also someone who helps you get better at a sport or lesson.
3 A **coach** can also be a kind of carriage.

coal

Coal is a black rock that is dug out of the ground. You can burn **coal** to get heat.

coast

The **coast** is the edge of the land where it meets the sea.

coat   coats

You wear a **coat** over your other clothes when you go outside.

cobweb   cobwebs

A **cobweb** is a thin net made by a spider. It catches flies and other insects.

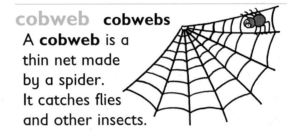

cocoa

1 Cocoa is a brown powder used to make chocolate. It is made from the seeds of a tree.
2 Cocoa is also a hot drink that tastes of chocolate.

coconut   coconuts

A **coconut** is a large nut with a hard hairy shell. Inside there is hard white flesh that you can eat and milky juice that you can drink.

cocoon   cocoons

A **cocoon** is a small ball that a caterpillar spins. A caterpillar lives inside a **cocoon** as it changes into a butterfly or moth.

a
b
Cc
d
e
f
g
h
i
j
k
l
m
n
o
p
q
r
s
t
u
v
w
x
y
z

coffee

Coffee is a hot drink. You make it by pouring hot water onto a powder made from **coffee** beans.

coin coins

A **coin** is a piece of metal money.

cold colder, coldest; colds

1 When you are **cold**, you want to put on more clothes.
My feet are as cold as ice!
2 If you catch a **cold**, you feel ill and your nose runs.
Mum has a bad cold and can't stop sneezing.

collar collars

1 The **collar** of a shirt or coat is the part around the neck. It often folds over. (See page 177.)
2 A **collar** is also the band you put round the neck of a dog or cat.
My dog Lottie has her name and address on her collar.

collect collects, collecting, collected

1 If you **collect** something, you go and fetch it.
My dad collected the parcel from the post office.
2 When you put special things of the same kind together, you **collect** them.
I collect coins from all over the world.

colour colours

Red, yellow and blue are all **colours**. You can mix them together to get other **colours**. (See page 184.)
Green is the colour you get when you mix yellow and blue.

column columns

1 A **column** is a tall, solid cylinder.
The building had lots of columns.

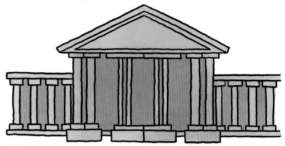

2 A **column** is a list of numbers or words. They go down a page one below the other.
The letters of the alphabet at the side of this page are in a column.

comb combs

A **comb** is a piece of plastic or metal with teeth. You use a **comb** to tidy your hair.

come comes, coming, came, come

1 When you **come** to a place, you arrive there.
When I came to school, the playground was nearly empty.
2 If someone asks you to **come**, they want you to go with them.

comfortable

Something **comfortable** feels nice to be in or to wear.
The chair was so comfortable that I fell asleep.

comic comics

A **comic** is a magazine for children. It tells stories in pictures.

comma commas

The punctuation mark , is a **comma**. It is used to make you stop very briefly when reading, like this, or in lists of things.

Nancy likes apples, oranges, pears and cherries.

commas

common

If something is **common**, you often see it. The opposite of **common** is rare.

compact disc compact discs

A **compact disc** is a flat, round, plastic object. It has music or information stored on it. It is also called a CD.

compare compares, comparing, compared

When you **compare** two things, you see how they are the same or different.

competition competitions

A **competition** is a test of who is best at something.

complete completes, completing, completed

1 If you **complete** something, you finish it.

We completed the jigsaw puzzle.

2 If something is **complete**, there is nothing left out.

Here is a complete list of the people in my class.

computer computers

A **computer** is a machine that stores and finds information. It can also do calculations, play games and control other machines.

concert concerts

A **concert** is a musical show.

Ania sang in the school concert.

cone cones

A **cone** has a circular top or bottom. Its other end comes to a point.

We love to eat ice cream cones!

confused

If you feel **confused**, you are not sure what to think or do.

conjunction conjunctions

A **conjunction** is a word that joins two parts of a sentence together. The words *and*, *but* and *or* are all **conjunctions**.

*I like cricket **and** football, **but** I don't like swimming **or** basketball.*

conker conkers

A **conker** is a shiny brown nut. It comes from a horse chestnut tree. You thread the nuts on string to play **conkers**.

a
b
Cc
d
e
f
g
h
i
j
k
l
m
n
o
p
q
r
s
t
u
v
w
x
y
z

a
b
Cc
d
e
f
g
h
i
j
k
l
m
n
o
p
q
r
s
t
u
v
w
x
y
z

consonant **consonants**
A **consonant** is any letter of the alphabet except for a, e, i, o, or u.

contain **contains, containing, contained**
Something **contains** the things that are inside it.
*My lunch box **contains** two sandwiches and an apple.*

container **containers**
A **container** is anything that you keep things in.

contents
The **contents** of something are the things inside it. The **contents page** of a book tells you what information is inside.

continue **continues, continuing, continued**
If you **continue** to do something, you keep on doing it.
*Please **continue** reading until you get to the bottom of the page.*

control **controls, controlling, controlled**
If you **control** something, you make it do what you want it to.

cook **cooks, cooking, cooked**
If you **cook** food, you make it ready to eat. You can fry, boil, bake or microwave it.

cooker **cookers**
A **cooker** is a machine for cooking food.

cool **cooler, coolest**
If you feel **cool**, you feel almost cold.
*On a hot day it is **cool** under the trees.*

copy **copies, copying, copied**
1 If you **copy** something, you make something that is exactly like it.
Copy the drawing into your book.
2 A **copy** of something looks exactly the same as it does.

corn
Cereal crops like wheat and oats are called **corn**.

corner **corners**
A **corner** is where two edges, sides or lines meet.
*A square has four **corners**.*
*Dad waited for me at the **corner** of the street.*

correct
If your answer is **correct**, you have not made any mistakes.

corridor **corridors**
A **corridor** is a long, narrow passage that leads to other rooms.

cost **costs, costing, cost**
1 If something **costs** an amount of money, that is what you pay for it.
2 The **cost** of something is what you must pay for it.

costume costumes

You wear a **costume** when you are pretending to be someone or something else.

Tom wore a costume in the school play.

cot cots

A **cot** is a bed for a baby. It has high sides to stop the baby from falling out of it.

cottage cottages

A **cottage** is a small house in the country.

cotton

1 Cotton is cloth made from the soft white seeds of a plant.

2 Cotton is also thread used to sew things together.

Mum used white cotton to sew on my name tapes.

cough coughs, coughing, coughed

When you **cough**, you clear your throat with a sudden loud noise.

could

If you **could** do something, you are able to do it or you were able to do it.

Molly could read when she was five.

See **can**.

count counts, counting, counted

1 If you **count**, you say numbers in the right order.

You count up to 100 and I'll hide.
Count back from 5 to 2.
Count on from 5 to 9.

2 When you **count** a group of things, you work out how many there are.

counter counters

1 A **counter** is a small round object. It is used in games that are played on a board.

2 In a small shop, you are served and pay your money at the **counter**.

country countries

1 A **country** is a land with its own people, language and laws.

Australia and Spain are countries.

2 The **country** is the land away from towns. You see farms, fields, trees and rivers in the **country**.

couple couples

1 A **couple** is two things of the same kind.

2 A **couple** is also two people who are married or going out together.

That young couple are about to get married.

cousin cousins

Your **cousin** is the son or daughter of your aunt or uncle.

a
b
Cc
d
e
f
g
h
i
j
k
l
m
n
o
p
q
r
s
t
u
v
w
x
y
z

a
b

Cc

d
e
f
g
h
i
j
k
l
m
n
o
p
q
r
s
t
u
v
w
x
y
z

cover **covers, covering, covered**

1 If you **cover** something, you put something else on it.
Harry covered his face with his hands.

2 A **cover** is something you put over or on another thing.
The cushion has a red cover.

cow **cows**

A **cow** is a large farm animal. You drink the milk that comes from **cows**.

crab **crabs**

A **crab** is an animal with a hard shell. It lives in the sea.

crack **cracks, cracking, cracked**

1 If you **crack** a plate, thin lines appear on it but it does not break.
2 A **crack** is the thin line on something that is **cracked**.
3 A **crack** is also a loud noise.

cracker **crackers**

1 A **cracker** is a paper tube that bangs when it is pulled apart. It often has a paper hat and a toy inside.
2 A **cracker** is also a thin biscuit.

crane **cranes**

1 A **crane** is a tall machine for lifting heavy objects.
2 A **crane** is a tall bird with a long neck and legs. It lives near water.

crash **crashes, crashing, crashed**

1 When something **crashes**, it hits something else suddenly and noisily.
2 A **crash** is the noise of something **crashing**.
I heard the crash of breaking glass.
3 When a computer **crashes**, it suddenly stops working.

crawl **crawls, crawling, crawled**

When you **crawl**, you move along on your hands and knees.
The baby crawled across the floor.

crayon **crayons**

A **crayon** is used for drawing in colour. **Crayons** can be coloured pencils or made of wax.

cream

Cream is the thick liquid from the top of milk.
We had strawberries and cream for tea.

creature **creatures**

A **creature** is any animal.

creep **creeps, creeping, crept**

If you **creep**, you move slowly and quietly.
I tried to creep silently up the stairs.

cricket

Cricket is a game played with a bat and a ball. There are two teams of eleven players.

cried See **cry**.

cries See **cry**.

crisp crisps; crisper, crispest
1 A **crisp** is a thin slice of dry, fried potato. It is eaten cold.
Alan passed around a packet of crisps.
2 Crisp food is firm and breaks easily.
This lettuce is nice and crisp.

crocodile crocodiles
A **crocodile** is a large reptile with strong teeth. It is similar to an alligator.

crop crops
A **crop** is something that farmers grow to sell.

cross crosses, crossing, crossed; crosser, crossest
1 When you **cross** something, you go to the other side of it.
2 A little mark like x or + is a **cross**.
3 A **cross** person is angry.

crowd crowds
A **crowd** is a lot of people in one place.

crown crowns
A **crown** is a ring of gold and jewels. Kings and queens wear **crowns** on their heads.

cruel crueller, cruellest
A **cruel** person enjoys hurting others.

crumb crumbs
A **crumb** is a tiny piece of bread or cake.

crunch crunches, crunching, crunched
If you **crunch** food, you break it up noisily between your teeth.

cry cries, crying, cried
1 When you **cry**, tears fall from your eyes.
2 If you **cry** out, you shout.
3 A **cry** is a shout.

cub cubs
A **cub** is a young wild animal such as a tiger, fox or bear.

cube cubes
A **cube** is a shape with six square faces that are all the same size. Sugar is sometimes made into **cubes**.

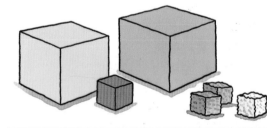

cucumber cucumbers
A **cucumber** is a long, thin vegetable with dark green skin.

a
b
Cc
d
e
f
g
h
i
j
k
l
m
n
o
p
q
r
s
t
u
v
w
x
y
z

a
b
Cc
d
e
f
g
h
i
j
k
l
m
n
o
p
q
r
s
t
u
v
w
x
y
z

cuddle **cuddles, cuddling, cuddled**
When you **cuddle** someone, you put your arms around them.
Dad cuddled the baby.

cup **cups**
1 A **cup** is a small round container with a handle. You drink tea or coffee from a **cup**.
2 You can also win a **cup** as a prize. This kind of **cup** is made of metal.

cupboard **cupboards**
A **cupboard** is a piece of furniture with a door. You keep things in it.

curl **curls, curling, curled**
1 A **curl** is a piece of curved hair.
2 When you **curl** up, you bend your body into a little ball.

curly **curlier, curliest**
If you have **curly** hair, the pieces of hair make curls or rings.
Lindsay has long curly hair.

curry **curries**
Curry is food cooked with different spices.
The vegetable curry was hot and spicy.

curtain **curtains**
A **curtain** is a piece of cloth that hangs by a window. You can pull it across to keep out the light.

curved
If a line, road or surface bends, it is **curved**.

cushion **cushions**
A **cushion** is a bag filled with something soft. It is comfortable to lean against or sit on.

customer **customers**
A **customer** is someone who buys something in a shop.

cut **cuts, cutting, cut**
1 When you divide something with a sharp blade, you **cut** it.
Angus cut his birthday cake.
Mum cut my dad's hair.
2 If you **cut** yourself, you break open your skin and make it bleed.
3 A **cut** is an opening or wound made by something sharp.

cylinder **cylinders**
A **cylinder** is a tube with circular ends. It can be solid or hollow.

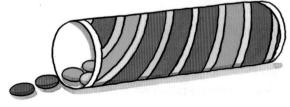

dad or daddy dads or daddies

Dad or **daddy** is what you call your father.

damage damages, damaging, damaged

When you **damage** something, you spoil it.

The cat scratched the chair and damaged it.

damp damper, dampest

If something is **damp**, it is a bit wet.

I've been drying my hair, but it still feels damp.

dance dances, dancing, danced

If you **dance**, you move in time to music.

danger dangers

If there is **danger**, something bad could happen.

Danger – thin ice!

dangerous

Something **dangerous** can hurt you.

dark darker, darkest

1 When it is **dark**, there is very little light or no light at all.

2 Dark hair is brown or black.

date dates

A **date** is the day, month and sometimes the year when something happens.

Today's date is the 18th of September.

daughter daughters

A person's **daughter** is their female child.

dawn

Dawn is the early morning, when it starts to get light.

We got up at dawn to go fishing.

day days

A **day** is made up of 24 hours. There are seven **days** in a week.

dead

If someone or something is **dead**, they are no longer alive.

deaf

A **deaf** person cannot hear well. Some **deaf** people cannot hear at all.

dear dearer, dearest

1 When you write a letter, you put **Dear** before the person's name.

2 Something **dear** is expensive.

December

December
December is the twelfth month of the year. It has 31 days.

decide decides, deciding, decided
You **decide** when you choose between two or more things.

deck decks
A **deck** is one of the floors of a ship or bus.
Tom sat on the top deck of the bus.

decorate decorates, decorating, decorated
1 If you **decorate** something, you make it look nice.
Mum and I decorated the cake with icing.
2 If you **decorate** a room, you paint it or paper the walls.

deep deeper, deepest
When something is **deep**, it is a long way down to its bottom.
Be careful! The water is very deep here.

deer deer
A **deer** is a large wild animal. The male **deer** may have horns called antlers.

defend defends, defending, defended
If you **defend** something, you protect it.

definition definitions
A **definition** tells you the meaning of a word. You find **definitions** in a dictionary.
The definition of "baby" is "a very young child".

delete deletes, deleting, deleted
If you **delete** something, you cross it out or remove it.

delicious
Food that is **delicious** smells and tastes lovely.

delighted
If you are **delighted**, you are very pleased.
Mum was delighted when I won the race.

deliver delivers, delivering, delivered
When you **deliver** something to someone, you take it to them.
The postman delivered the parcel to our house.

den dens
1 A **den** is the home of some wild animals. Bears, foxes and lions live in **dens**.
2 A **den** is also a secret place where children meet.

dentist dentists
A **dentist** looks after people's teeth.

depth
The **depth** of something is how deep it is.

describe describes, describing, described
When you **describe** something, you say what it is like.

description descriptions
The words that tell you about something are its **description**.
Sonia gave a description of the burglar to the police.

desert deserts
A **desert** is a hot, dry place. There is so little water that almost nothing grows.

desk desks
A **desk** is a special table for working on. It sometimes has drawers to keep things in.

dessert desserts
A **dessert** is fruit or a sweet food served at the end of a meal. It can also be called a pudding.

destroy destroys, destroying, destroyed
If you **destroy** something, you damage it so much that it can never be used again.
The car was destroyed by fire.

diagram diagrams
A **diagram** is a drawing. It shows or explains how something works.

diamond diamonds
A **diamond** is a hard bright jewel. It looks like clear glass.
My granny has a ring with a diamond in it.

diary diaries
A **diary** is a book with a space for every day in the year. You write what happens in it.

dice
Dice are small cubes with numbers or spots on each face, usually from one to six.

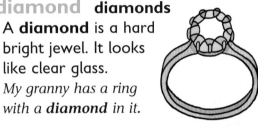

dictionary dictionaries
A **dictionary** is a book that lists words in alphabetical order. It tells you how to spell them and what they mean.

did See **do**.

didn't
Didn't is short for did not.

die dies, dying, died
When people, animals and plants **die**, they stop living.

a
b
c
Dd
e
f
g
h
i
j
k
l
m
n
o
p
q
r
s
t
u
v
w
x
y
z

a
b
c
Dd
e
f
g
h
i
j
k
l
m
n
o
p
q
r
s
t
u
v
w
x
y
z

difference   differences

1 A **difference** between two things is what is not the same about them.
2 The **difference** between two numbers is the answer you get when you take the smaller number away from the larger number.
*The **difference** between 5 and 3 is 2.*

different

1 When two or more things are **different**, they are not the same.
2 If something is **different**, it has changed in some way.
*Your hair looks **different** – have you had it cut?*

difficult

Something **difficult** is hard to do or to understand.
*These puzzles are very **difficult**.*

dig   digs, digging, dug

When you **dig** soil or sand, you use your hands or a spade to pick it up and move it.

digit   digits

A **digit** is a symbol used to write numbers. There are ten different **digits** in our number system:
0, 1, 2, 3, 4, 5, 6, 7, 8 and 9.
*In the number 47, the **digits** are 4 and 7. 47 is a two-**digit** number.*

digital

A **digital** watch or clock has no hands. It gives the time in numbers.

dinner   dinners

Dinner is the main meal of the day. It is sometimes the evening meal. Some people call the midday meal **dinner**.

dinner time

Dinner time is the time of day when you usually eat your dinner.

dinosaur   dinosaurs

Dinosaurs were huge animals that lived on Earth 65 million years ago.
(See pages 172–173.)

dip   dips, dipping, dipped

When you **dip** something, you put it in liquid briefly.
*Mary **dipped** her toe in the water.*

direction   directions

1 If you are moving in a certain **direction**, that is the way you are going.
2 **Directions** are instructions about how to get somewhere.

dirt

Dirt is anything that makes things not clean, such as dust or mud.

dirty   dirtier, dirtiest

Something **dirty** has dirt on it.
*My shoes were **dirty** after playtime.*

disappear **disappears, disappearing, disappeared**

If something **disappears**, it suddenly goes out of sight.

*The car **disappeared** around the corner.*

disappointed

You are **disappointed** when something that happens is not as good as you hoped.

*I was very **disappointed** when our team lost the match.*

disaster **disasters**

A **disaster** is something very bad that happens, causing damage and death. An air crash or an earthquake is a **disaster**.

disc **discs**

A **disc** is a flat circular piece of anything.

discover **discovers, discovering, discovered**

If you **discover** something, you find out about it or see it for the first time.

discuss **discusses, discussing, discussed**

You **discuss** something when you talk about it with other people.

disguise **disguises**

You wear a **disguise** so that people will not know who you are.

*Is that Hamish wearing a **disguise?***

dish **dishes**

A **dish** is a plate or bowl for food.

dishwasher **dishwashers**

A **dishwasher** is a machine that washes dirty plates, cups and saucepans.

disk **disks**

Disk is another way of spelling disc.

distance **distances**

The **distance** between two things is how far it is between them.

*The **distance** between Richard and Caroline is about 3 metres.*

disturb **disturbs, disturbing, disturbed**

When you **disturb** someone, you stop them doing what they are doing.

*Please don't **disturb** me – I'm trying to read.*

dive **dives, diving, dived**

If you **dive**, you jump head first into water. You hold your arms straight above your head.

*Sadiya **dived** off the top board.*

a
b
c
Dd
e
f
g
h
i
j
k
l
m
n
o
p
q
r
s
t
u
v
w
x
y
z

a
b
c

Dd

e
f
g
h
i
j
k
l
m
n
o
p
q
r
s
t
u
v
w
x
y
z

divide **divides, dividing, divided**
If you **divide** something, you share it into equal groups.
*You can **divide** 6 sweets into 3 groups of 2.*

6 ÷ 3 = 2

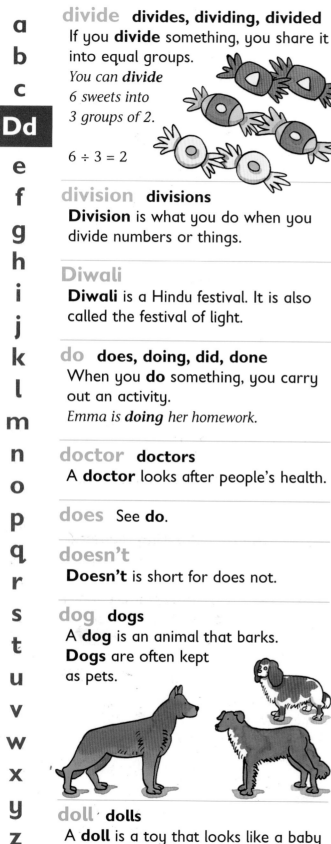

division **divisions**
Division is what you do when you divide numbers or things.

Diwali
Diwali is a Hindu festival. It is also called the festival of light.

do **does, doing, did, done**
When you **do** something, you carry out an activity.
*Emma is **doing** her homework.*

doctor **doctors**
A **doctor** looks after people's health.

does See **do**.

doesn't
Doesn't is short for does not.

dog **dogs**
A **dog** is an animal that barks.
Dogs are often kept as pets.

doll **dolls**
A **doll** is a toy that looks like a baby or small person.

dolphin **dolphins**
A **dolphin** is a mammal that lives in the sea. It looks like a fish with a large nose.

domino **dominoes**
A **domino** is a flat rectangular block used for playing a game. It has up to six spots on each half.

done See **do**.

donkey **donkeys**
A **donkey** is an animal rather like a small horse. It has long ears.

don't
Don't is short for do not.
*I really **don't** like rice pudding!*

door **doors**
A **door** is a piece of wood, metal or glass that closes the way into a building, room or piece of furniture.
*Liam opened the front **door**.*

doorbell **doorbells**
A **doorbell** is a bell on the outside of a house. You ring it to tell the people inside that you are there.

dot **dots**
A **dot** is a very small round mark.
*You put a **dot** over the letter i.*

double **doubles, doubling, doubled**

1 If you **double** something, you multiply it by two. You can also add two of the same numbers together.
6 × 2 and 6 + 6 are both ways of finding double 6.
2 If something is **double** the size, it is twice as big.

downstairs

If you go **downstairs**, you go down to a lower floor.
Let's go downstairs to play.

drag **drags, dragging, dragged**
When you **drag** something, you pull it along the ground.

dragon **dragons**
In stories, a **dragon** is a pretend animal with wings and claws. It can breathe out fire.

drain **drains**
A **drain** is a pipe to carry liquid like bath water away.

drank See **drink**.

draw **draws, drawing, drew, drawn**
1 When you **draw**, you make a picture using pencil, crayons or chalk. You can also **draw** on a computer screen using a mouse.
2 When a game ends in a **draw**, the two sides have the same score.

drawer **drawers**
A **drawer** is a box that slides in and out of a piece of furniture. You keep things in **drawers**.

drawing **drawings**
A **drawing** is a picture made with a pen or pencil.
See **draw**.

drawn See **draw**.

dream **dreams, dreaming, dreamed or dreamt**
When you **dream**, thoughts and pictures come into your mind while you are asleep.

dress **dresses, dressing, dressed**
1 When you **dress**, you put on your clothes.
2 A **dress** is a piece of clothing worn by a girl or woman. It covers her from her shoulders to her legs.

dressing gown **dressing gowns**
A **dressing gown** is a piece of clothing. It is like a coat and you wear it over your night clothes. (See page 176.)

drew See **draw**.

a
b
c
Dd
e
f
g
h
i
j
k
l
m
n
o
p
q
r
s
t
u
v
w
x
y
z

a
b
c

Dd

e
f
g
h
i
j
k
l
m
n
o
p
q
r
s
t
u
v
w
x
y
z

drink **drinks, drinking, drank, drunk**
1 When you **drink**, you put liquid into your mouth and swallow it.
2 A **drink** is a liquid that you swallow.
*Would you like a **drink** of milk?*

drip **drips, dripping, dripped**
When liquid **drips**, it falls in small drops.

drive **drives, driving, drove, driven**
1 When you **drive** a car, you make it go where you want it to.
2 A **drive** is a journey in a car.

drop **drops, dropping, dropped**
1 When you **drop** something, you let it fall.
*The dog **dropped** the stick.*
2 A **drop** is a very small amount of liquid.

drove See **drive**.

drown **drowns, drowning, drowned**
If someone **drowns**, they die under water because they cannot breathe.

drum **drums**
A **drum** is a musical instrument that you hit to make a sound.

drunk See **drink**.

dry **drier or dryer, driest**
Something **dry** has no liquid on it.

duck **ducks**
A **duck** is a bird that can swim and fly. It lives near water.

dug See **dig**.

dull **duller, dullest**
1 **Dull** means not clear or bright.
2 **Dull** also means boring.

dungeon **dungeons**
A **dungeon** is a dark, underground prison beneath a castle.

dusk
Dusk is the time just before it gets dark in the evening.

dust
Dust is a dry, fine powder. It is carried on the air.

dustbin **dustbins**
A **dustbin** is a large metal or plastic container for rubbish.

duvet **duvets**
A **duvet** is a large cloth bag filled with something soft. You sleep under it to keep warm.

dying See **die**.

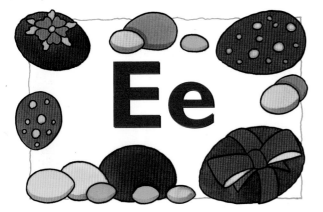

each

Each means every one of a number of things or people.
*Give **each** child two pencils.*

eagle eagles

An **eagle** is a large bird with a curved beak. It lives among mountains.

ear ears

Your **ears** are on each side of your head. Your **ears** help you to hear. (See page 174.)

early earlier, earliest

1 If you are **early**, you arrive before you are expected.
2 The **early** part of something is near the beginning.
*I play football in the **early** morning.*

earn earns, earning, earned

You **earn** money by working for it.
*I **earned** some pocket money by washing the car.*

earring earrings

An **earring** is a piece of jewellery that you wear on your ear.

earth

1 The planet **Earth** is the world we live on.

2 The soil that plants grow in is also called **earth**.

earthquake earthquakes

When there is an **earthquake**, the ground shakes suddenly. Sometimes buildings fall down.

east

East is the direction you look in to see the sun rise.

Easter

Easter is a spring festival when Christians remember Jesus Christ coming back from the dead.

easy easier, easiest

Something **easy** is simple to do or understand.
*The sums were much **easier** than I expected.*

eat eats, eating, ate, eaten

When you **eat** something, you put it into your mouth and swallow it.
*I'm going to **eat** my apple at playtime.*

echo echoes

You hear an **echo** when a sound that you make comes back to you.
*Anil shouted his name in the cave and heard the **echo**.*

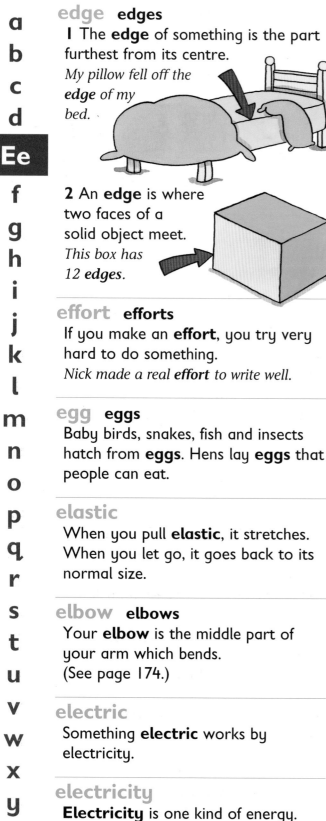

a
b
c
d
Ee
f
g
h
i
j
k
l
m
n
o
p
q
r
s
t
u
v
w
x
y
z

edge edges

1 The **edge** of something is the part furthest from its centre.
My pillow fell off the edge of my bed.

2 An **edge** is where two faces of a solid object meet.
This box has 12 edges.

effort efforts

If you make an **effort**, you try very hard to do something.
Nick made a real effort to write well.

egg eggs

Baby birds, snakes, fish and insects hatch from **eggs**. Hens lay **eggs** that people can eat.

elastic

When you pull **elastic**, it stretches. When you let go, it goes back to its normal size.

elbow elbows

Your **elbow** is the middle part of your arm which bends.
(See page 174.)

electric

Something **electric** works by electricity.

electricity

Electricity is one kind of energy. It is used to give heat and light and to make machines work.

elephant elephants

An **elephant** is a very large land animal. It has a long nose called a trunk.

e-mail or email

e-mails or emails
An **e-mail** is a message that you send from one computer to another.

emerald emeralds

An **emerald** is a green jewel.

empty emptier, emptiest

If something is **empty**, there is nothing in it.

encyclopedia or encyclopaedia

encyclopedias or encyclopaedias
An **encyclopedia** is a book or CD with information on lots of different things.

end ends, ending, ended

1 The **end** of something is where it finishes.
We walked to the end of the street.
2 Something **ends** when it stops happening.
The film ends at eight o'clock.

ending endings

The **ending** is the last part of something.
The story had a sad ending.

enemy enemies

An **enemy** is someone who fights against you or your country.

energetic

An **energetic** person is full of life and always active.

energy

Energy is the power that makes things happen. People need **energy** to move and do things. Machines need **energy** to make them work. Electricity is one kind of **energy**.

engine engines

An **engine** is a machine that makes things like cars and trains move.

enjoy enjoys, enjoying, enjoyed

If you **enjoy** doing something, you like doing it and it makes you happy.

enormous

Enormous means very large.

enough

Something that is **enough** is as much as you need or want.

*Has Meena had **enough** to eat?*

enter enters, entering, entered

1 If you **enter** a place, you go into it.
2 If you **enter** something on a computer, you key it in.

entrance entrances

An **entrance** is the way into a place.

envelope envelopes

An **envelope** is a paper cover for a letter.

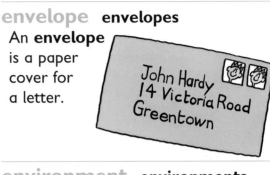

John Hardy
14 Victoria Road
Greentown

environment environments

The **environment** is the air, water and land around us.

equal equals, equalling, equalled

1 If two things are **equal**, they are the same size or number.
*One week is **equal** to seven days.*
2 Equals means that two numbers or quantities are the same.
The symbol = means **equals**.
$5 - 1 = 4$

equipment

Equipment is the set of things needed for something or to do something.
*Miss Jones got out the PE **equipment**.*

escape escapes, escaping, escaped

If you **escape** something, you get away from it.
*The animals **escaped** from the burning forest.*

estimate estimates, estimating, estimated

1 If you **estimate** the answer to something, you make a careful guess.
2 An **estimate** is a careful guess.

a
b
c
d
Ee
f
g
h
i
j
k
l
m
n
o
p
q
r
s
t
u
v
w
x
y
z

51

a
b
c
d
Ee
f
g
h
i
j
k
l
m
n
o
p
q
r
s
t
u
v
w
x
y
z

even
1 If a number is **even**, it can be divided exactly by two.
2 Even also means flat and smooth.

evening   evenings
Evening is the last part of the day. It starts to get dark and you go to bed.

ever
Ever means at any time.
*Have you **ever** been to France?*

every
Every means each one of a number of things or people.
*Give **every** girl a hat and **every** boy a cap.*

everybody
Everybody means every person.
*Has **everybody** given me their homework?*

everyone
Everyone is another word for everybody.

everything
Everything means all the things.
*Have you put **everything** away?*

everywhere
Everywhere means every place.
*The dog followed her **everywhere**.*

evil
An **evil** person is very bad.

exact
An **exact** answer cannot be any better or closer.

exactly
If you say a number or time **exactly**, it is not less or more than that.
*I cut the cake into **exactly** three pieces.*

example   examples
You use an **example** to show what you mean.
*Tom's picture is a good **example** of how to use paint.*

excellent
Something **excellent** is very good.
*Gill's work was **excellent**.*

except
Except means not including someone or something.
*Everyone got a sweet **except** me.*

exchange   exchanges, exchanging, exchanged
If you **exchange** something, you give it away and receive something else instead.
*I **exchanged** my book for a different one.*

excited

If you are **excited**, you are so happy that you want to jump about.
*I'm really **excited** about my birthday!*

exclaim   exclaims, exclaiming, exclaimed

If you **exclaim**, you cry out suddenly.
*"Ouch! That hurt!" Dad **exclaimed**.*

exclamation mark
exclamation marks

A mark like ! is an **exclamation mark**. It is used to show that someone exclaims.
I can't wait until my birthday!

excuse   excuses

An **excuse** is a reason you give for doing or not doing something.
*You're late. What is your **excuse**?*

exercise   exercises

1 Exercise is anything active that you do to keep fit.

2 An **exercise** is a set of questions that help you practise something.
*Practise your tables by doing **Exercise** 5 for homework.*

exit   exits

An **exit** is a way out of a place.
*The **exit** is blocked and I can't get out.*

expect   expects, expecting, expected

If you **expect** something to happen, you believe it will happen.
*Dan's the fastest, so I **expect** him to win.*

expensive

Something **expensive** costs a lot.

explain   explains, explaining, explained

If you **explain** something, you say what it means or why it happened.

explanation   explanations

An **explanation** says what something means or why it happened.

explode   explodes, exploding, exploded

When something **explodes**, it blows up into small pieces with a loud bang.

explore   explores, exploring, explored

If you **explore** a place, you look around to see what it is like.

extinct

An animal that is **extinct** has died out. There will never be any more of them.
*Dinosaurs are **extinct**.*

extra

Something **extra** is more than usual.
*My mum gave me **extra** pocket money.*

eye   eyes

Your **eyes** are parts of your face. You see with your **eyes**.
(See page 174.)

a
b
c
d
e
Ff
g
h
i
j
k
l
m
n
o
p
q
r
s
t
u
v
w
x
y
z

Ff

face faces
1 Your **face** is the front of your head. (See page 174.)
2 A **face** of a solid object is any one of its surfaces. *A cube has six faces.*

fact facts
A **fact** is something that is true. *It is a fact that the Earth goes round the Sun.*

factory factories
Things are made in a **factory**, usually using machines.

fail fails, failing, failed
You **fail** if you try to do something but cannot do it. *I tried to ring Anna, but I failed.*

fair fairer, fairest; fairs
1 A **fair** person treats everyone the same.
2 A person who is **fair** is beautiful. *"Mirror, mirror, on the wall, Who is the fairest of them all?"*
3 Someone with **fair** hair has pale hair.
4 A **fair** is an outdoor show that moves from town to town. *I went on an exciting ride at the fair.*

fairy fairies
In stories, a **fairy** is a very small person. **Fairies** have wings and magic powers. *Zina is dressed as a fairy.*

fairy tale fairy tales
A **fairy tale** is a story where magical things happen.

fall falls, falling, fell, fallen
1 If something **falls**, it drops towards the ground. *The apples fell from the tree onto the grass.*
2 If you **fall** asleep, you go to sleep.

false
Something is **false** when it is not true or is not real. *The clown wore a false nose.*

family families
Your parents, brothers, sisters, grandparents, aunts, uncles and cousins are your **family**.

famous
Someone **famous** is very well known. *Dick King-Smith is a famous writer.*

fantastic
If you say something is **fantastic**, you mean that it is wonderful.

far farther or further, farthest or furthest
Far means a long way. *Are you going far?*

farm farms

A **farm** is a place in the country where a farmer grows food or keeps animals.

farmer farmers

A **farmer** lives on a farm. **Farmers** grow food and look after animals.

fast faster, fastest; fasts, fasting, fasted

1 Something **fast** moves very quickly.
2 If you **fast**, you do not eat any food.

fasten fastens, fastening, fastened

When you **fasten** something, you fix one thing firmly to another.
*Please **fasten** your seat belt.*

fat fatter, fattest

1 A **fat** person or animal has a round, heavy body.
*Our dog is **fat**. She can't fit into her kennel.*
2 Fat is a food.
Butter is a kind of **fat**.

father fathers

A **father** is a man who has a son or daughter.

fault

It is your **fault** if you cause something bad to happen.
*It's John's **fault** the plant died, because he forgot to water it.*

favourite

Your **favourite** is the one you like best.
*Blue is my **favourite** colour.*

fax faxes

You use a **fax** to send a copy of a letter or picture to someone.

fear fears, fearing, feared

1 If you **fear** someone or something, they frighten you.
2 Fear is the nasty feeling you get when you are afraid.
*My mum has a **fear** of spiders.*

feast feasts

A **feast** is a large, special meal for lots of people.

feather feathers

Feathers cover the body of a bird. They are very light.

February

February is the second month of the year. It usually has 28 days. In a leap year, it has 29 days.

feed feeds, feeding, fed

When you **feed** a person or animal, you give them food.
*Did you **feed** the dog?*

feel feels, feeling, felt

1 When you **feel** happy, you are happy at that moment.
2 When you touch something to find out what it is like, you **feel** it.

feet See foot.

a
b
c
d
e
Ff
g
h
i
j
k
l
m
n
o
p
q
r
s
t
u
v
w
x
y
z

fell See **fall**.

felt See **feel**.

female females
A **female** person or animal can be a mother. Girls and women are **females**.

fence fences
A **fence** is a kind of wall around a garden or field. It is made from wood or wire.

ferry ferries
A **ferry** is a kind of boat. It carries people and vehicles across a river or a narrow piece of sea.

festival festivals
1 A **festival** is a number of special shows. A **festival** is often held every year.
2 A **festival** is also a special time, like Christmas or Diwali.
We all bring fruit and vegetables to school for our Harvest Festival.

fetch fetches, fetching, fetched
If you **fetch** something, you go and get it from another place.
I fetched my bike from the shop.

fete or **fête** fetes or fêtes
A **fete** is an outdoor show. There are competitions and things to eat and drink.
We went to the school fete on Saturday.

fever fevers
A **fever** is an illness that makes you very hot.

few fewer, fewest
Few means not many.
There are only a few seats left.

fiction
Fiction is stories that have been made up about people or animals that are not real.

field fields
A **field** is a piece of land on a farm. It has a fence or hedge around it.

fierce fiercer, fiercest
A **fierce** animal is very angry and likely to attack.
The fierce dog barked angrily.

fight fights, fighting, fought
When people or animals **fight**, they try to hurt each other.

figure figures
A **figure** is another word for a number or an amount.

fill fills, filling, filled
When you **fill** something, you use up the space inside it.
Mum filled my glass with orange juice.

film **films**

1 A **film** is a story shown on a screen using moving pictures.

2 You put a roll of **film** in your camera to take pictures.

fin **fins**

A **fin** is part of a fish. It helps the fish to travel through the water.

find **finds, finding, found**

1 When you see something that you are looking for, you **find** it.
2 When you **find** out about something, you learn something new. *Today we are going to **find** out about the weather.*

fine **finer, finest**

1 Something that is **fine** is very good. *A **fine** day is sunny and dry.*
2 Fine can also mean that something is very thin, like a line or a thread.

finger **fingers**

You have five **fingers** on each hand. (See page 174.)

finish **finishes, finishing, finished**

When you **finish** something, you come to the end of it, use it up or do the last part of it.

fire **fires**

1 Fire is the heat and light given off when things burn.
2 People have a **fire** to keep warm.

fire brigade **fire brigades**

A **fire brigade** is a group of firefighters. People call the **fire brigade** to put out a dangerous fire.

fire engine **fire engines**

A fire brigade travels in a **fire engine**.

firefighter **firefighters**

A **firefighter** puts out dangerous fires.

firework **fireworks**

When someone lights a **firework**, it sends out bright, coloured lights.

firm **firmer, firmest**

Something that is **firm** does not move easily when you push it.

first

When someone or something is **first**, they come before all the others. *January is the **first** month of the year.*

fish **fish or fishes**

A **fish** is an animal that lives under water. **Fish** are covered with scales.

a
b
c
d
e
Ff
g
h
i
j
k
l
m
n
o
p
q
r
s
t
u
v
w
x
y
z

a
b
c
d
e

Ff

g
h
i
j
k
l
m
n
o
p
q
r
s
t
u
v
w
x
y
z

fisherman **fishermen**
A **fisherman** is someone who catches fish.

fit **fits, fitting, fitted; fitter, fittest**
1 If something **fits**, it is the right size and shape.
2 If you are **fit**, you feel healthy and well.

fix **fixes, fixing, fixed**
1 If you **fix** something that was broken, you mend it.
*Dad managed to **fix** his car.*
2 If you **fix** two things together, you join them to each other.

flag **flags**
A **flag** is a rectangle of cloth with a coloured pattern on it. It flies from a pole. Every country in the world has its own **flag**.

flame **flames**
A **flame** is a hot, bright tongue of fire.

flap **flaps, flapping, flapped**
Something that **flaps** is joined to something on one side and moves backwards and forwards.
*The bird **flapped** its wings.*

flash **flashes**
A **flash** is a short, sudden, bright light.
*A **flash** of lightning lit up the sky.*

flat **flatter, flattest; flats**
1 A **flat** surface has no bumps or slopes.
2 A **flat** is a home on one floor. It is part of a bigger building.

flavour **flavours**
The **flavour** of food or drink is what it tastes like.
*I love ice cream – chocolate is my favourite **flavour**.*

flew See **fly**.

flies See **fly**.

flip **flips, flipping, flipped**
If you **flip** something, you turn it quickly and suddenly.
*Nadia **flipped** over the page.*

float **floats, floating, floated**
1 Something that **floats** in a liquid does not sink. It stays on top.
*The plastic duck **floated** on the water.*

2 Something that **floats** through the air moves slowly without getting lower.
*The balloon **floated** across the sky.*

flock **flocks**
A **flock** is a group of birds, sheep or goats.
*A **flock** of birds flew overhead.*

flood **floods**
There is a **flood** when water covers an area that is usually dry.
Boats came to rescue people from the flood.

floor **floors**
1 The **floor** of a room is the part you walk on.
I have a blue carpet on my bedroom floor.
2 A **floor** is all the rooms on the same level in a building.
Gran's flat is on the sixth floor.

floppy disk **floppy disks**
A computer can store information on a **floppy disk**.

flour
Flour is a white or brown powder made from wheat. It is used to make bread and cakes.

flow **flows, flowing, flowed**
If a liquid **flows**, it moves from place to place.
A river flows through our town.

flower **flowers**
A **flower** is a part of a plant. It makes seeds. Some **flowers** have coloured petals.

fly **flies, flying, flew, flown**
1 If you **fly**, you travel through the air.
2 A **fly** is a small flying insect.

fog
Fog is thick cloud that is near the ground. It makes it difficult to see.

foggy
When it is **foggy**, it is difficult to see because of the fog.

fold **folds, folding, folded**
If you **fold** something, you bend it over on itself.
Susan folded up her towel.

follow **follows, following, followed**
If you **follow** someone, you move along behind them.
We all followed Emma to the hall.

food **foods**
Food is anything that people and animals eat to stay alive. **Food** gives you the energy to do things.
My favourite food is fish fingers.

foot **feet**
1 Your **foot** is at the end of your leg. (See page 174.)
2 A **foot** is an older way to measure length.

football **footballs**
Football is a game played by two teams. They try to kick a **football** into a goal. Another word for **football** is soccer.

a b c d e **Ff** g h i j k l m n o p q r s t u v w x y z

a
b
c
d
e
Ff
g
h
i
j
k
l
m
n
o
p
q
r
s
t
u
v
w
x
y
z

footprint footprints
Footprints are the marks your feet leave when you walk in snow or wet sand.

forehead foreheads
Your **forehead** is the top of your face. (See page 174.)

foreign
Something that is **foreign** comes from another country.
*My family eats **foreign** food from all over the world.*

forest forests
A **forest** is a place where lots of trees grow together.

forgave See **forgive**.

forget forgets, forgetting, forgot, forgotten
If you **forget** something, you do not remember it.
*I **forgot** it was Mum's birthday.*

forgive forgives, forgiving, forgave, forgiven
If you **forgive** someone, you stop being angry with them.
*Mum **forgave** me for breaking her watch.*

forgot See **forget**.

forgotten See **forget**.

fork forks
A **fork** is a tool with sharp points and a handle. You use a **fork** to help you eat your food.

fortnight fortnights
A **fortnight** is the same as two weeks.

forwards
1 If you walk **forwards**, you are going in the direction that is in front of you.
2 Forwards is the opposite way to backwards. If you say the alphabet **forwards**, you start at A and finish at Z.

fossil fossils
A **fossil** is a plant or animal that has turned to stone. A **fossil** has been in the ground for many thousands of years.

fought See **fight**.

found See **find**.

fountain fountains
A **fountain** is a jet of water that shoots up into the air.

fox foxes
A **fox** is a wild animal that looks like a dog. It has a thick tail.

fraction fractions

A **fraction** is part of a whole number or shape. A half ($\frac{1}{2}$) and a quarter ($\frac{1}{4}$) are both **fractions**.

$\frac{1}{2}$ $\frac{1}{4}$

frame frames

A **frame** is the wood, metal or plastic around a picture or a window.

freckle freckles

Freckles are tiny brown spots on a person's skin.

free

1 If you are **free**, you can choose where you go and what you do.
2 Something that is **free** does not cost any money.
The supermarket gave away free balloons.

freeze freezes, freezing, froze, frozen

1 Water **freezes** when it gets very cold. It changes from water into ice.
2 If you are **freezing**, you are very, very cold.

fresh fresher, freshest

1 When something is **fresh**, it is new and clean.
Turn to a fresh page.
2 **Fresh** food is not old or bad.
3 **Fresh** water is not salty from the sea. It is rain water that has collected in a river or lake.

Friday Fridays

Friday is the day of the week between Thursday and Saturday.

fridge fridges

A **fridge** is a machine that keeps food cold and fresh.
Fridge is short for refrigerator.

fried See **fry**.

friend friends

A **friend** is a person you know well and like very much.
I play with my best friend every day.

friendly friendlier, friendliest

A **friendly** person is kind and easy to get on with.

fries

Fries are thin chips.
See **fry**.

frighten frightens, frightening, frightened

1 If you **frighten** someone, you make them afraid.
2 If you are **frightened**, you feel afraid.
My dog is frightened of loud noises.

frog frogs

A **frog** is a small animal that can swim and jump.
Frogs live on land and in water.

a
b
c
d
e
Ff
g
h
i
j
k
l
m
n
o
p
q
r
s
t
u
v
w
x
y
z

a
b
c
d
e

Ff

g
h
i
j
k
l
m
n
o
p
q
r
s
t
u
v
w
x
y
z

front

The **front** of something is the part that you usually see first.
*The driver sits at the **front** of the bus.*

frost **frosts**

There is a **frost** when it gets very cold. The ground is covered with thin white ice called **frost**.

frown **frowns, frowning, frowned**

When you **frown**, you look angry or worried. Lines appear on your forehead.
*Mum **frowned** when I banged the door.*

froze See **freeze**.

frozen See **freeze**.

fruit **fruit or fruits**

Fruit is the part of a plant that holds the seeds. Apples, oranges and bananas are **fruit** that you eat.

fry **fries, frying, fried**

If you **fry** food, you cook it in hot oil or fat.

full **fuller, fullest**

If something is **full**, there is no space left inside it.
*The bucket is **full** of sand.*

full stop **full stops**

A **full stop** is a punctuation mark. It looks like a dot and is used at the end of a sentence.

fun

When you have **fun**, you have a good time.
*We had a lot of **fun** at the circus.*

funny **funnier, funniest**

1 Something **funny** makes you laugh.
*The clowns were really **funny**.*
2 If something is **funny**, it can be strange in some way.
*Will gave me a **funny** look.*

fur

Fur is the thick, soft hair that grows on the bodies of animals. Bears, rabbits and cats have **fur**.

furniture

Chairs, tables and beds are **furniture**.

furry **furrier, furriest**

Something **furry** is covered in thick, soft hair.

further

Further is another word for farther. See **far**.

furthest

Furthest is another word for farthest. See **far**.

future

The **future** is the time that has not come yet.
*Yesterday was in the past, and tomorrow is in the **future**.*

Gg

gale gales
A **gale** is a very strong wind.
The fence was blown down in the gale.

game games
A **game** is something you play for fun, like hide-and-seek. Sports like football are **games** – so is a board **game** like Snakes and Ladders.

gap gaps
A **gap** is an empty space between two things.
Mick has a gap where his tooth fell out.

garage garages
1 A **garage** is a building where you keep a car.
2 You also buy petrol and have your car mended at a **garage**.

garden gardens
A **garden** is a piece of land next to a house. People grow flowers and vegetables in their **gardens**.

gas gases
1 **Gas** is something that is not solid or liquid. Air is a **gas**.
2 You burn **gas** to heat your home and cook your food.

gate gates
A **gate** is a kind of door in a fence or wall.

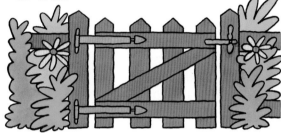

gather gathers, gathering, gathered
When you **gather** things, you bring them together in one place.
The teacher gathered up the books.

gave See **give**.

geese See **goose**.

gentle gentler, gentlest
If you are **gentle**, you are kind and careful.
The nurse was very gentle with the baby.

gentleman gentlemen
Gentleman is a polite word for a man.

gerbil gerbils
A **gerbil** is a small animal that looks like a mouse. **Gerbils** are often kept as pets.

a
b
c
d
e
f
Gg
h
i
j
k
l
m
n
o
p
q
r
s
t
u
v
w
x
y
z

a
b
c
d
e
f

Gg

h
i
j
k
l
m
n
o
p
q
r
s
t
u
v
w
x
y
z

get **gets, getting, got**
If you **get** something, you fetch it from somewhere.
*It's cold, so I'll **get** my jumper.*

ghost **ghosts**
A **ghost** looks like a person who is already dead. Some people say they have seen a **ghost**.

giant **giants**
1 In fairy stories, a **giant** is a very large, strong person.
2 Something very big is called **giant**.
*This is a **giant** packet of cornflakes.*

gigantic
Something **gigantic** is very, very large.
*The boys ate a **gigantic** meal.*

giggle **giggles, giggling, giggled**
If you **giggle**, you keep on laughing.
*We couldn't stop **giggling** – it was such a good joke!*

giraffe **giraffes**
A **giraffe** is a tall animal with a very long neck.

girl **girls**
A **girl** is a child who will grow up to be a woman.
*Your mum used to be a **girl**.*

give **gives, giving, gave, given**
If you **give** something to someone, you let them have it.
*Sam **gave** Raul an apple.*

glad
When you are **glad**, you are pleased and happy.
*I'm really **glad** Gran's coming to stay.*

glass **glasses**
1 **Glass** is a hard, clear material that you can see through. Windows and bottles are made of **glass**.
2 A **glass** is a kind of cup made of **glass**.

glasses **glasses**
You wear **glasses** to help you see better. You look through two special pieces of glass or plastic held in a frame.

gloomy **gloomier, gloomiest**
1 If you are **gloomy**, you feel sad.
2 **Gloomy** weather is cloudy and rather dark.

glove **gloves**
You wear **gloves** on your hands to keep them warm. **Gloves** have a separate part for each finger.

glue

You use **glue** to stick things together.
*Ben stuck the picture in his book with **glue**.*

go goes, going, went, gone
If you **go** somewhere, you move from one place to another.
*My brother and I are **going** to the swimming pool.*

goal goals
1 You must put the ball in the **goal** to score a point in a game like football.
*The crowd roared when the ball shot into the **goal**.*
2 You score a **goal** by putting the ball into the **goal**.
*Mark scored a **goal** with a brilliant header.*

goat goats
A **goat** is a farm animal. **Goats** are kept for their milk.

gold

Gold is a shiny yellow metal. It is used to make jewellery.

golden

Something **golden** is the colour of gold.
*Goldilocks had **golden** hair.*

goldfish goldfish
A **goldfish** is a small golden or orange fish. People keep **goldfish** as pets.

gone See **go**.

good better, best
1 If you think something is **good**, you like it.
*That was a **good** game!*
2 If you are **good** at something, you can do it well.
*Jack is very **good** at reading.*
3 A **good** person is kind to others and cares about them.

goodbye

You say **goodbye** to someone when you leave them.

good night

You say **good night** to someone when they go to bed.

goose geese
A **goose** is a large bird that swims and flies.

gorilla gorillas
A **gorilla** is the largest ape. It has thick black fur and is very strong.

got See **get**.

a b c d e f **Gg** h i j k l m n o p q r s t u v w x y z

a
b
c
d
e
f

Gg

h
i
j
k
l
m
n
o
p
q
r
s
t
u
v
w
x
y
z

grab **grabs, grabbing, grabbed**
If you **grab** something, you take hold of it quickly.
Grab your things! We're going swimming.

gram **grams**
You can measure mass in **grams**. There are 1000 **grams** (g) in a kilogram (kg).

grammar
Grammar is the rules of a language. It tells you how words and sentences should be put together.

grandad **grandads**
Grandad is another word for grandfather.

grandfather **grandfathers**
Your **grandfather** is the father of your father or mother.

grandmother **grandmothers**
Your **grandmother**, or **gran**, is the mother of your father or mother.

granny **grannies**
Granny is another word for grandmother.

grape **grapes**
A **grape** is a juicy fruit that grows in a bunch.

grapefruit **grapefruits**
A **grapefruit** is a juicy yellow fruit like a big orange. People eat **grapefruit** for breakfast.

graph **graphs**
A **graph** is a special kind of drawing or diagram that shows information.

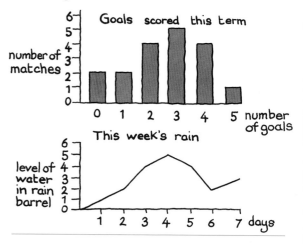

grass
Grass is a plant with thin green leaves. It grows in fields and gardens. Cows and other animals eat **grass**.

great **greater, greatest**
1 **Great** means very good.
We had a great time at the fair!
2 **Great** also means very large.
There's a great black cloud up above us.
3 **Great** can also mean important or famous.
Victoria was a great queen.

greedy **greedier, greediest**
A **greedy** person takes more than they need.

grew See **grow**.

groan groans, groaning, groaned

If you **groan**, you make a long, low sound. You **groan** when something hurts or upsets you.

Mum groaned when she saw the mess.

ground

1 The **ground** is what you walk on.

The plate hit the ground with a crash.

2 Ground also means earth or land.

The ground was too hard to dig.

group groups, grouping, grouped

1 A **group** of people or things is a number of them that are all together.

2 If you **group** people or things, you put them together.

grow grows, growing, grew, grown

When something **grows**, it gets bigger.

growl growls, growling, growled

A **growl** is a deep, rough, angry sound made in the throat.

The lion growled angrily.

grown See **grow**.

grown-up grown-ups

A **grown-up** is a person who is not a child. **Grown-ups** are called adults.

guard guards, guarding, guarded

1 If you **guard** something, you watch over it to keep it safe.

2 A **guard** is a person who **guards** someone or something.

guess guesses

If you give an answer when you are not sure it is right, you are making a **guess**.

guide guides, guiding, guided

1 If you **guide** someone, you show them the way to go.

2 A **guide** shows you around somewhere, or leads the way.

We followed the guide through the jungle.

guinea pig guinea pigs

A **guinea pig** is a small, furry animal without a tail. It is often kept as a pet.

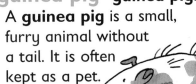

guitar guitars

A **guitar** is a musical instrument with strings. You play it with your fingers.

gun guns

A **gun** is a machine that fires bullets.

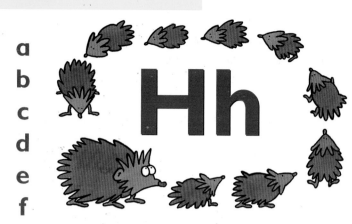

Hh

a
b
c
d
e
f
g
Hh
i
j
k
l
m
n
o
p
q
r
s
t
u
v
w
x
y
z

had   See **have**.

hail

Hail is drops of hard, icy rain.
*The **hail** bounced off the road.*

hair   **hairs**
Your **hair** is what
grows on your head.
It is made up of lots
of **hairs**.
*Stacey has curly
red **hair**.*

hairy   **hairier, hairiest**
Something covered in hair is **hairy**.

half   **halves**
I If you divide
something
equally into
two, each
part is a **half**.
2 When you say the time, **half** past
means 30 minutes past.
*Mum's coming home at **half** past two.*

halfway
If you are **halfway** between two
places, you are the same distance
from each of them.

hall   **halls**
I The **hall** of a house is just inside
the front door.
2 A **hall** can also be a large room or
building.
*Assembly is held in the school **hall**.*

Halloween
Halloween is the 31st of October.
Children like to dress up in costumes.

halve   **halves, halving, halved**
If you divide something exactly in
two, you **halve** it.

halves   See **half**.

hammer   **hammers**
A **hammer** is a tool used for hitting
nails into wood.

hamster   **hamsters**
A **hamster** is a small, furry animal
that looks like a mouse
without a tail.
It is often kept
as a pet.

hand   **hands, handing, handed**
I Your **hand** is at the end of your
arm. (See page 174.)
2 If you **hand** something to
someone, you give it to them.

handle   **handles**
The **handle** of anything is the part
that you hold in your hand.
*Alice turned the **handle** and opened the
front door.*

handlebars

Handlebars are part of a bicycle. (See page 175.)

handwriting

Your **handwriting** is the writing you do with a pen or pencil.

hang   hangs, hanging, hung

If you **hang** something, you fix it at the top.

*Please **hang** your coat up.*

Hanukkah or Chanukah

Hanukkah is an eight-day Jewish festival of lights.

happen   happens, happening, happened

If something **happens**, it takes place.

happy   happier, happiest

When you are **happy**, you are very pleased.

*I was so **happy** on my birthday!*

harbour   harbours

Boats are tied up in a **harbour** to keep them safe from big waves.

hard   harder, hardest

1 Something that is **hard** is firm or difficult to break.

*This ice cream is as **hard** as a rock!*

2 Something that is **hard** to do is difficult.

*I can't do this puzzle – it's really **hard**!*

hare   hares

A **hare** is an animal that looks like a large rabbit. It has long ears and long back legs.

harvest   harvests

The **harvest** is the gathering of crops when they are ripe.

*At **harvest** time, the corn is cut and taken to the barn.*

has   See **have**.

hat   hats

A **hat** is something you wear on your head.

hatch   hatches, hatching, hatched

When a baby bird **hatches**, it comes out of its egg.

hate   hates, hating, hated

If you **hate** something, you do not like it at all.

have   has, having, had

1 If you **have** something, you own it or it is with you.

*Fred **has** a new bike.*

2 If you **have** done something, you did it in the past.

*I **have** been on an aeroplane before.*

a
b
c
d
e
f
g

Hh

i
j
k
l
m
n
o
p
q
r
s
t
u
v
w
x
y
z

haven't

Haven't is short for have not.
*I **haven't** done it yet – I'll do it tomorrow.*

hay

Hay is dry grass that is used to feed animals.

head heads

1 Your **head** is the top part of your body. (See page 174.)
2 The **head** of something is the person in charge.
*The **head** teacher called everyone into the hall.*

headache headaches

A **headache** is a pain in the head that goes on hurting.

headlight headlights

Headlights are the lights at the front of a car. (See page 175.)

head teacher head teachers

The **head teacher** is the teacher in charge of a school.

heal heals, healing, healed

When something **heals**, it becomes healthy again.

healthy healthier, healthiest

If you are **healthy**, your body is fit and you are not ill.

hear hears, hearing, heard

When you **hear** something, you notice the sound it makes.
*I can **hear** music.*

heart hearts

Your **heart** is inside your chest. It sends blood round your body.

heat heats, heating, heated

1 If you **heat** something, you make it warmer.
*I'll **heat** some soup for lunch.*
2 **Heat** is the warm feeling you get from something hot.

heaven

Heaven is a place of happiness. Some people think you go to **heaven** when you die.

heavy heavier, heaviest

A person or thing that is **heavy** weighs a lot.

hedge hedges

A **hedge** is a kind of fence between fields or gardens. It is made of small trees and bushes.

hedgehog hedgehogs

A **hedgehog** is a small brown animal with sharp spines on its back. It rolls into a ball when it is frightened.

heel   heels
1 Your **heel** is the back part of your foot. (See page 174.)
2 A **heel** is also part of a shoe.

height   heights
You measure how high something is to find out its **height**.

held   See **hold**.

helicopter   helicopters
A **helicopter** is a vehicle that flies. It has large blades on top which spin round. **Helicopters** can go straight up into the air.

helmet   helmets
A **helmet** is a hard hat that keeps your head from getting hurt.
*You should always wear a **helmet** when you ride your bike.*

help   helps, helping, helped
When you **help** someone, you do something useful for them.
*I **helped** Dad carry the bags.*

hen   hens
A **hen** is a female chicken. **Hens** lay eggs that people can eat.

her
Her means belonging to a girl or woman.
*Mum's coming. I can see **her** car.*

herd   herds, herding, herded
1 A **herd** is a group of animals of one kind that live together.
*There is a large **herd** of cows on this farm.*

2 If you **herd** animals or people, you move them together as a group.
*The dogs **herded** the sheep into a corner.*

here
Here means the place where you are now.
*Have you seen my skateboard? I thought I left it **here**.*

hero   heroes
1 A **hero** is a man or boy who has done something brave or good.
2 The **hero** of a story is the man or boy that it is about.

heroine   heroines
1 A **heroine** is a woman or girl who has done something brave or good.
2 The **heroine** of a story is the woman or girl that it is about.

hexagon   hexagons
A **hexagon** is a flat shape that has six sides.

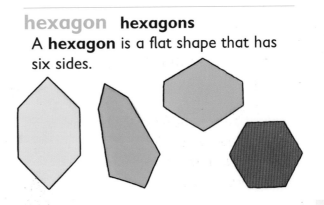

a
b
c
d
e
f
g
Hh
i
j
k
l
m
n
o
p
q
r
s
t
u
v
w
x
y
z

hide **hides, hiding, hid, hidden**
I If you **hide** something, you put it where no one can find it.
2 If you **hide**, you go where no one can see you.

high **higher, highest**
If something is **high**, it is tall or a long way from the ground.

hill **hills**
A **hill** is land that is higher than the land around it. A **hill** is not as tall as a mountain.

hip **hips**
Your **hip** is where your leg joins your body. (See page 174.)

hippopotamus

hippopotamuses or hippopotami
A **hippopotamus**, or **hippo** for short, is a very large African animal. It lives in or near a river.

his

His means belonging to a boy or a man.
*Dan can't find **his** books.*

history

Things that happened in the past are **history**.
*We learned about the Romans in our **history** lesson.*

hit **hits, hitting, hit**
If you **hit** something, you touch it very hard.
*The ball **hit** me so hard that I fell over.*

hive **hives**
When people keep bees, the bees live in a **hive**.

hold **holds, holding, held**
I You **hold** something by taking it in your hand.
*My friend asked me if I would like to **hold** his pet hamster.*
2 A container **holds** the amount you can fit inside it.
*This jar **holds** 50 sweets.*

hole **holes**
A **hole** is an opening or empty space in something.
*There is a **hole** in my jumper.*

holiday **holidays**
If you are on **holiday**, you do not have to go to school or work. You may go away for a **holiday**.
*We are going camping for our **holiday** this year.*

hollow

Something **hollow** has space inside it.
*Owls sometimes build their nests in **hollow** trees.*

holly

Holly is a small tree or bush. It has prickly green leaves and red berries.

home homes

Your **home** is the place where you live.
*My **home** is near the school.*

honest

If you are **honest**, you tell the truth and people trust you.

honey

Honey is a sweet, sticky food made by bees.

hoof hoofs or hooves

A **hoof** is the hard, bony part of a horse's foot. Cows, sheep and goats have **hooves**, too.

hop hops, hopping, hopped

1 When you **hop**, you jump on one foot. When birds **hop**, they jump with both feet together.
2 A **hop** is a small jump.

hope hopes, hoping, hoped

When you **hope** that something will happen, you want it to happen.
*I **hope** I pass the test!*

horn horns

A **horn** is the hard point that sticks out from the heads of some animals.

horrible

If you think something is **horrible**, you do not like it at all.
*Today's pudding was **horrible**!*

horse horses

A **horse** is a large animal that people ride. Some **horses** pull things, and some take part in races.

hospital hospitals

A **hospital** is a large building where ill people are looked after.

hot hotter, hottest

Something **hot** is very warm. Very **hot** things can burn you.
*Be careful! The water is very **hot**.*

a b c d e f g **Hh** i j k l m n o p q r s t u v w x y z

a
b
c
d
e
f
g

Hh

i
j
k
l
m
n
o
p
q
r
s
t
u
v
w
x
y
z

hotel hotels
You can stay in a **hotel** when you are away from home. A **hotel** has lots of bedrooms.

hour hours
An **hour** is made up of 60 minutes. There are 24 **hours** in a day.

house houses
A **house** is a building that people live in. It has several rooms.

how
When you say **how** something happens, you explain the way that it happens.

huge
If something is **huge**, it is very, very big.
An elephant is a huge animal.

human humans
A **human** is a person.

hump humps
A **hump** is a big bump. Camels have **humps**.

hundred hundreds
A **hundred** is the number 100. The number 342 has 3 **hundreds**, 4 tens and 2 units.

hung See **hang**.

hungry hungrier, hungriest
When you are **hungry**, you want something to eat.
I'm hungry! I haven't eaten for hours.

hunt hunts, hunting, hunted
1 When an animal **hunts**, it chases and kills another animal.
Owls hunt for mice at night.
2 When you **hunt** for something, you look everywhere for it.
I'm hunting for my socks.

hurry hurries, hurrying, hurried
If you **hurry**, you move or do something quickly.
We were late, so we hurried to school.

hurt hurts, hurting, hurt
If something **hurts**, you feel pain there.
My arm hurts where I banged it.

husband husbands
A **husband** is a married man.

hut huts
A **hut** is a small building. It is usually made of wood.

hutch hutches
A **hutch** is a kind of cage made from wood and metal. Pet rabbits live in **hutches**.

ii

ice

Ice is water that has frozen hard.
*Would you like some **ice** in your drink?*

ice cream   ice creams

Ice cream is a sweet, frozen food. It tastes creamy and comes in lots of flavours.

icicle   icicles

An **icicle** is a pointed, hanging piece of ice. It is made when dripping water freezes.
Icicles were hanging from the roof.

idea   ideas

An **idea** is something you have thought of yourself.
*I had a brilliant **idea**!*

igloo   igloos

An **igloo** is a kind of house. It is made from blocks of hard snow or ice.

ill

When you are **ill**, you do not feel very well.
*Kyle was **ill**, so he spent the day in bed.*

illness   illnesses

If you have an **illness**, you do not feel well. Colds and flu are **illnesses**.

illustration   illustrations

An **illustration** is a picture in a book.

illustrator   illustrators

An **illustrator** is someone who draws the pictures in a book.

imagine   imagines, imagining, imagined

If you **imagine** something, you picture it in your mind.

immediately

If something happens **immediately**, it happens straight away.
*Stop that noise **immediately**!*

important

1 If something is **important**, it matters a lot.
*Good health is **important**.*
2 An **important** person has a lot of power.
*A president is an **important** person.*

a
b
c
d
e
f
g
h
Ii
j
k
l
m
n
o
p
q
r
s
t
u
v
w
x
y
z

impossible

If something is **impossible**, it cannot be done.

It is impossible to walk on water.

in

I If someone or something is **in** a place, they are there.

The PE mats are in the cupboard.

2 If you are **in**, you are at home.

inch inches

In the past, **inches** were used to measure length.

index indexes

An **index** is an alphabetical list at the back of a book. It tells you where to find things in the book.

Index		
ant	3,10	hedgehog 15
anteater	4,8	hyena 17
antelope 5		lion 8
bear	7,18	monkey 21
camel 9		otter 19
crocodile 10		owl 5
dolphin	6,13	snake 7,29
elephant 2		tortoise 19
flamingo 6		walrus 12
gazelle 25		zebra 32

information

Information about something or someone is the facts about them.

Have you any information about hot-air balloons?

initial initials

An **initial** is the first letter of a word or name.

Sam Brown's initials are S.B.

ink inks

Ink is a coloured liquid. It is used for printing or writing.

insect insects

An **insect** is a tiny animal with six legs. **Insects** usually have wings. Flies and ants are **insects**.

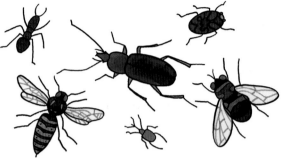

inside insides

The **inside** of something is surrounded by the rest of it.

Open the box and look inside it!

instruction instructions

Instructions are words or drawings that tell you what to do.

I followed the instructions on the packet.

instrument instruments

I An **instrument** is a tool people use to do a job.

The doctor used an instrument to look down my ear.

2 You play a musical **instrument** to make music. Recorders and violins are musical **instruments**.

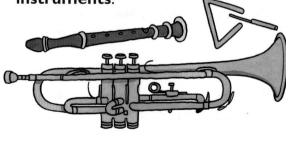

interesting

If something is **interesting**, you want to know more about it.
*The film was so **interesting** that we watched it again.*

Internet

You can look things up on the **Internet** using a computer.

interrupt   interrupts, interrupting, interrupted

If you start talking when someone is speaking, you **interrupt** them.
*Don't **interrupt** – let Ellie finish what she is saying!*

invent   invents, inventing, invented

If you **invent** something, you are the first person to think of it.
*Alexander Graham Bell **invented** the telephone.*

investigate   investigates, investigating, investigated

If you **investigate** something, you try to find out all about it.
*We are **investigating** what happens when you mix different colours.*

invisible

If something is **invisible**, you cannot see it.
*The school was **invisible** from the road.*

invitation   invitations

You get an **invitation** when someone asks you to their party.

invite   invites, inviting, invited

If you **invite** someone to a party, you ask them to come to it.

iron   irons

1 Iron is a strong, hard, grey metal.
2 People use a hot **iron** to smooth clothes.

island   islands

(*sounds like* eye-land) An **island** is a piece of land that has water all around it.

its

Its means belonging to it.
*My bike has lost **its** wheel.*

it's

It's is short for it is or it has.
__It's__ an interesting book.
__It's__ stopped raining now.

a
b
c
d
e
f
g
h
i
Jj
k
l
m
n
o
p
q
r
s
t
u
v
w
x
y
z

jacket jackets
A **jacket** is a short coat.

jam jams
1 Jam is a sweet food. It is made from fruit and sugar.
*I had strawberry **jam** on my toast.*
2 There is also a **jam** when it is so crowded that nothing can move.
*The car was stuck in a traffic **jam**.*

January
January is the first month of the year. It has 31 days.

jar jars
A **jar** is a glass container with a wide top. It is used for storing food, such as jam.

jaw jaws
Your **jaw** is one of the bones that hold your teeth.

jeans
Jeans are trousers made from a strong cotton material. They are often blue. (See page 176.)

jelly jellies
Jelly is a soft, sweet food that you can see through.

jet jets
1 A **jet** is an aeroplane that can fly very fast and very high.
2 A **jet** is also a narrow stream of something.
*A **jet** of water shot out through the hole in the pipe.*

jewel jewels
A **jewel** is a beautiful, shiny stone that costs a lot of money. Diamonds and emeralds are **jewels**.

jewellery
Rings, necklaces and earrings are **jewellery**. **Jewellery** is often made of gold or silver, sometimes with jewels.

jigsaw jigsaws
A **jigsaw** is a puzzle. You fit together shapes to make a picture.
*This **jigsaw** has 100 pieces.*

job jobs
1 A **job** is something you have to do.
*It's my **job** to collect the books.*
2 A **job** is also work that you are paid to do.
*My mum has a **job** as a bus driver.*

join joins, joining, joined
1 When you **join** things, you put them together.

2 If you **join** a club, you become a member of it.
*Sophie has **joined** the swimming club.*

joint joints
A **joint** is a part of the body where two bones fit together.
*Your finger **joints** are called knuckles.*

joke jokes
A **joke** is something that you say to make people laugh.

journey journeys
If you go on a **journey**, you travel from one place to another.

jug jugs
A **jug** is a container for holding liquids. It has a handle and a lip for pouring.

juice juices
Juice is the liquid that can be squeezed out of fruit.
*I drink orange **juice** at breakfast.*

July
July is the seventh month of the year. It has 31 days.

jump jumps, jumping, jumped
You **jump** when you move yourself into the air.
*Tim **jumped** off the wall.*

jumper jumpers
A **jumper** is a piece of clothing with sleeves. You wear it on the top half of your body to keep you warm.

June
June is the sixth month of the year. It has 30 days.

jungle jungles
A **jungle** is a thick forest in a hot country.

just
If something has **just** happened, it happened a very short time ago.
*I **just** got to school a minute ago.*

a
b
c
d
e
f
g
h
i
Jj
k
l
m
n
o
p
q
r
s
t
u
v
w
x
y
z

79

a b c d e f g h i j

Kk

l m n o p q r s t u v w x y z

kangaroo kangaroos
A **kangaroo** is a large Australian animal. It jumps on its strong back legs. Female **kangaroos** carry their babies in a pocket on their stomachs.

keep keeps, keeping, kept
1 If you **keep** something, you save it.
I'll keep the last sweet for you.
2 If you **keep** something somewhere, you always put it there.
I keep all my books in the bookcase.

kennel kennels
A **kennel** is a small shed for a dog to sleep in.

kept See **keep**.

ketchup
Ketchup is a cold sauce made from tomatoes.

kettle kettles
People boil water in a **kettle**.

key keys, keying, keyed
1 A **key** is a piece of metal with a special shape. It opens a lock.
2 You press the **keys** on a piano or a computer with your fingers.
3 If you **key** in information on a computer keyboard, you type it in.

keyboard keyboards
A **keyboard** is all the keys on a computer or piano.

kick kicks, kicking, kicked
If you **kick** something, you hit it hard with your foot.
Malik kicked the ball into the air.

kid kids
1 A **kid** is a young goat.
2 Children are often called **kids**.

kill kills, killing, killed
If somebody **kills** something, they make it die.
The fox killed the chicken.

kilogram or kilo
kilograms or kilos
You can measure mass in **kilograms** or **kilos**. A **kilogram** (kg) is 1000 grams.

kilometre kilometres
You can measure distance in **kilometres**. A **kilometre** (km) is 1000 metres.

kind kinder, kindest; kinds
1 A **kind** person is caring and helpful.
It was kind of Harry to lend me his bike.
2 Things of the same **kind** are part of the same group.
Cars and bikes are kinds of vehicles.

king kings
A **king** is a man who rules a country because he belongs to a royal family.

kingdom **kingdoms**
A **kingdom** is the area that is ruled by a king or queen.

kiss **kisses, kissing, kissed**
When you **kiss** someone, you touch them with your lips.
Mum kissed me on the cheek.

kitchen **kitchens**
A **kitchen** is a room where food is cooked.

kite **kites**
A **kite** is a toy that you fly in the air. It is tied to a long piece of string.

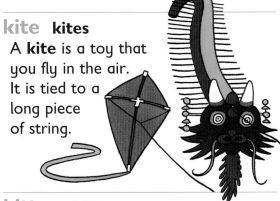

kitten **kittens**
A **kitten** is a young cat.

knee **knees**
Your **knee** is the part of your leg that bends. (See page 174.)

kneel **kneels, kneeling**
knelt or kneeled
When you **kneel**, you get down on your knees.

knew See **know**.

knickers
Knickers are pants worn by women and girls. (See page 176.)

knife **knives**
A **knife** is a tool for cutting things. It has a handle and a sharp blade.

knight **knights**
Hundreds of years ago, a **knight** was a soldier who wore armour and rode a horse.

knit **knits, knitting, knitted**
When you **knit**, you make clothes using wool and a pair of long needles.

knives See **knife**.

knock **knocks, knocking, knocked**
1 If you **knock** something, you hit it hard.
2 If you **knock** on a door, you make a noise to tell people you are there.

knot **knots**
A **knot** is made by tying two pieces of string together.

know **knows, knowing, knew, known**
1 If you **know** something, it is in your mind and you do not need to learn it.
2 If you **know** someone, you have met them before.

koala **koalas**
A **koala** is a small Australian animal.

a
b
c
d
e
f
g
h
i
j
Kk
l
m
n
o
p
q
r
s
t
u
v
w
x
y
z

a
b
c
d
e
f
g
h
i
j
k
Ll
m
n
o
p
q
r
s
t
u
v
w
x
y
z

label **labels**
A **label** is a small notice that tells you more about something.

lace **laces**
1 Lace is another word for shoelace.
2 Lace is also a kind of pretty cloth with lots of holes in it.

ladder **ladders**
You climb up a **ladder** to reach something high. **Ladders** are made of metal or wood.

lady **ladies**
Lady is a polite word for a woman.

ladybird **ladybirds**
A **ladybird** is a small red beetle with black spots. It is often found in gardens.

laid See **lay**.

lain See **lie**².

lake **lakes**
A **lake** is a large area of fresh water with land all around it.

lamb **lambs**
A **lamb** is a young sheep.

lamp **lamps**
You turn on a **lamp** to give you light when it is dark.

land **lands, landing, landed**
1 When you **land** somewhere, you arrive after a journey by aeroplane.
*We **landed** at the airport.*
2 Land is the dry part of the Earth not covered by water.

lane **lanes**
A **lane** is a narrow road.

language **languages**
Language is the words people use to speak and write. People in different countries speak different **languages**.

lap **laps, lapping, lapped**
1 When you sit down, the tops of your legs make your **lap**.
*The cat likes to sit on my **lap**.*
2 An animal **laps** when it drinks using its tongue.
*The cat **lapped** up its milk.*

large larger, largest
If something is **large**, it is big.
Katie and I shared a large drink.

last lasts, lasting, lasted
1 When something is **last**, it comes at the end.
The last month of the year is December.
2 If something **lasts**, it goes on for some time.
This film lasts an hour.

late later, latest
1 If you are **late**, you arrive after you are expected.
2 The **late** part of something is near the end.
We'll get there by late afternoon.

laugh laughs, laughing, laughed
When you **laugh**, you make a sound to show that something is funny.
We all laughed at the clown.

law laws
A **law** is a rule that everyone in a country must follow.
Dropping litter is against the law.

lawn lawns
A **lawn** is the grass that grows next to a house.

lay lays, laying, laid
1 If you **lay** something down, you put it down carefully.
Please lay your pencils down on the table.
2 If you **lay** the table, you get it ready for a meal.
3 When a hen **lays** an egg, it pushes it out of its body.
See **lie²**.

layer layers
A **layer** is something flat that goes above or below something else.
Mum covered the carpet with a layer of newspaper.

lazy lazier, laziest
A **lazy** person does not want to work.
I feel too lazy to get out of bed!

lead leads, leading, led
1 (*sounds like* seed) If you **lead** someone, you go in front of them to show the way.
You lead and we'll follow.
2 (*sounds like* seed) If you **lead** in a race, you are in front of the other runners.
Joe was leading the others until the last few metres.
3 (*sounds like* seed) A **lead** is a long piece of leather that you fix to a dog's collar.
4 (*sounds like* red) **Lead** is a heavy, soft grey metal.
5 (*sounds like* red) The **lead** of a pencil is the part which makes marks.

leader leaders
The **leader** of a group is in charge of it.
The captain is the leader of the team.

a
b
c
d
e
f
g
h
i
j
k
Ll
m
n
o
p
q
r
s
t
u
v
w
x
y
z

a
b
c
d
e
f
g
h
i
j
k
Ll
m
n
o
p
q
r
s
t
u
v
w
x
y
z

leaf **leaves**
A **leaf** is a flat, green part of a tree or plant. **Leaves** grow out of branches or stems.

lean **leans, leaning, leaned, leant**
If you **lean**, you bend in one direction.
*That tree **leans** over the road.*

leap **leaps, leaping, leapt or leaped**
1 If you **leap**, you jump a long way.
*Megan **leapt** across the stream.*
2 In a **leap year**, February has 29 days instead of 28.

learn **learns, learning, learned, learnt**
When you **learn** something, you get to know something new.
*I am **learning** to ride a bike.*

least
Least means the smallest amount.
*Sarah and Ian ate most of the popcorn – I had the **least**.*

leather
Leather is made from the skin of animals. Shoes and bags can be made of **leather**.

leave **leaves, leaving, left**
1 When you **leave** a place, you go away from it.
2 If you **leave** something somewhere, you do not take it with you.

leaves See **leaf** and **leave**.

led See **lead**.

left
Left is the opposite of right. When you read or write, you start at the **left** side of the page.
*Tom has his **left** foot on the ball.*

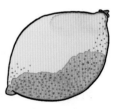

leg **legs**
Your **legs** are parts of your body. (See page 174.)

lemon **lemons**
A **lemon** is a small yellow fruit. It has a very sharp flavour.

lemonade
Lemonade is a cold drink that is made from lemons, sugar and water.

lend **lends, lending, lent**
When someone **lends** you something, they give it to you for a short time. Then you give it back.
*Please will you **lend** me your pencil sharpener?*

length **lengths**
You measure how long something is to find out its **length**.

lent See **lend**.

less

Less means not as much.

*If you have a large drink and I have a small drink, I have **less** than you.*

lesson   lessons

A **lesson** is a time when you are taught something.

*I had a swimming **lesson** today.*

let   lets, letting, let

If someone **lets** you do something, they say you may do it.

*Nicky **let** me ride her bicycle.*

letter   letters

1 A **letter** is a written message.
*I wrote a **letter** to my granny in Australia.*
2 A **letter** is one of the symbols you use to write words.
*A B C D are capital **letters** and a b c d are lower-case **letters**.*

lettuce   lettuces

Lettuce is a green vegetable. Its leaves are often used in salad.

level

If something is **level**, it is flat.
*A table needs to be **level**.*

library   libraries

A **library** is a place where lots of books are kept. You can borrow books from a **library** to read at home.

lick   licks, licking, licked

If you **lick** something, you move your tongue across it.
*The dog **licked** the bowl clean.*

lid   lids

A **lid** is a cover on a container. You take off the **lid** to open the container.
*Tim took the **lid** off the pan.*

lie^1 lies, lying, lied

If you **lie** or tell a **lie**, you say something which you know is not true.

lie^2 lies, lying, lay, lain

If you **lie** down, you rest your body flat on something.
*Our cat **lies** in the sun all day.*

life   lives

Your **life** is the time when you are alive. The **life** of a person or animal begins when they are born and ends when they die.

lifeboat   lifeboats

A **lifeboat** is a boat that goes to save people who are in danger at sea.

lift   lifts, lifting, lifted

1 If you **lift** something, you pick it up and move it upwards.
*I'll **lift** that heavy box for you.*
2 A **lift** carries people up and down in a building.

a
b
c
d
e
f
g
h
i
j
k
Ll
m
n
o
p
q
r
s
t
u
v
w
x
y
z

85

a
b
c
d
e
f
g
h
i
j
k
Ll
m
n
o
p
q
r
s
t
u
v
w
x
y
z

light lights, lighting, lit; lighter, lightest

1 **Light** comes from the sun during the day.

2 A **light** is a lamp that you turn on to help you see when it is dark.

3 If you **light** something, you make it start to burn.

4 Something **light** is not heavy.

5 A **light** colour is pale.

lighthouse lighthouses

A **lighthouse** is a tower with a bright, flashing light at the top. It warns ships of dangerous rocks.

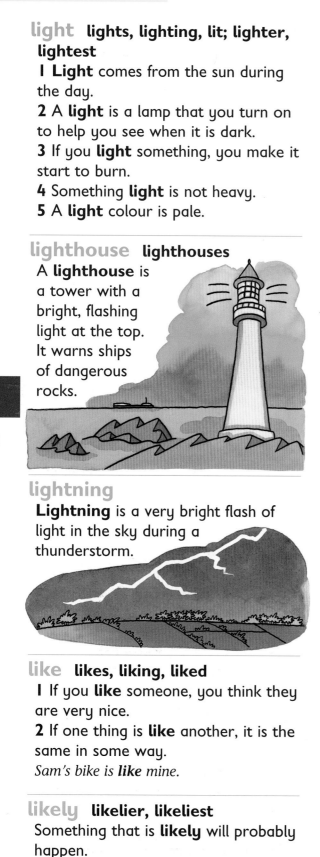

lightning

Lightning is a very bright flash of light in the sky during a thunderstorm.

like likes, liking, liked

1 If you **like** someone, you think they are very nice.

2 If one thing is **like** another, it is the same in some way.

*Sam's bike is **like** mine.*

likely likelier, likeliest

Something that is **likely** will probably happen.

*Susie works hard, so she's **likely** to do well.*

line lines

1 A **line** is a long, thin mark. **Lines** can be straight or curved.

*Put a **line** under the date.*

2 A **line** is also a row of people or things.

*We wait in a **line** for our dinner.*

lion lions

A **lion** is a large wild cat. It eats other animals.

lip lips

Your **lips** are the parts of your face around your mouth. (See page 174.)

liquid liquids

A **liquid** is something that pours easily and is not solid. Water, milk, oil and fruit juice are all **liquids**.

list lists

If you make a **list**, you write things down one after another.

*Mum wrote the things she needed on a shopping **list**.*

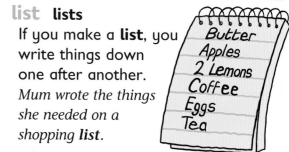

Butter
Apples
2 Lemons
Coffee
Eggs
Tea

listen listens, listening, listened

When you **listen**, you try to hear something.

lit See **light**.

litre litres

You can measure liquid in **litres**.

A **litre** (l) is 1000 millilitres (ml).

*Can I have a **litre** of milk, please?*

litter

Litter is rubbish that people drop on the ground.

Please take your litter home with you.

little   **less, least**

1 If something is **little**, it is small.

Grandad gave some milk to the little kitten.

2 A **little** means only a small amount.

Grandad only gave the kitten a little milk.

live   **lives, living, lived**

1 If you **live,** you are alive and breathing.

2 If you **live** in a place, your home is there.

David lives in Wales.

lives   See **life** and **live**.

lizard   **lizards**

A **lizard** is a reptile with four legs and a long tail. **Lizards** have rough, dry skins.

load   **loads, loading, loaded**

When you **load** a vehicle, you put lots of things on it or in it.

We loaded the car with suitcases.

loaf   **loaves**

You can cut a **loaf** of bread into slices. Some **loaves** are already sliced.

local

If something is **local**, it is near to your home.

I go to the local school.

lock   **locks, locking, locked**

1 If something is **locked**, you need a key to open it.

2 A **lock** keeps a door or suitcase shut. It can only be opened with the right key.

log   **logs**

A **log** is a large piece of wood from a tree.

lollipop   **lollipops**

A **lollipop** is a hard sweet on a stick. It is also called a lolly.

lolly   **lollies**

1 **Lolly** is another word for lollipop.

2 A **lolly** is also a piece of flavoured ice or ice cream on a stick.

lonely   **lonelier, loneliest**

If you are **lonely**, you are unhappy because you are alone.

My gran gets lonely, so I often go to see her.

long   **longer, longest**

1 Something **long** is a great distance from end to end.

2 A **long** time is a great amount of time. **Long** ago means many years ago.

a
b
c
d
e
f
g
h
i
j
k
Ll
m
n
o
p
q
r
s
t
u
v
w
x
y
z

a
b
c
d
e
f
g
h
i
j
k
Ll
m
n
o
p
q
r
s
t
u
v
w
x
y
z

look looks, looking, looked
1 If you **look** at something, you turn your eyes towards it so you can see it.
*I **looked** at my dirty hands.*
2 If you **look** for something, you try to find it.
*Peter **looked** everywhere for his coat.*

loose looser, loosest
Something that is **loose** moves about.
*Sasha has a **loose** tooth.*

lorry lorries
A **lorry** is a large vehicle. It carries big things by road.

lose loses, losing, lost
1 If you **lose** something, you cannot find it.
*I've **lost** my book. I don't know where it is!*
2 If you **lose** a race, you do not come first.

lost
If you are **lost**, you do not know where you are.
*We were **lost**, so we asked the way.*
See **lose**.

lot lots
A **lot** means a large number or amount.
*There are a **lot** of boys in my class.*

loud louder, loudest
Something **loud** is very noisy.
*The music got **louder** as the band came up the road.*

love loves, loving, loved
1 **Love** is a very strong feeling of liking for someone.
2 If you **love** someone, you like them very, very much.

lovely lovelier, loveliest
Something **lovely** is very nice to see, hear, smell or do.
*That music is **lovely**!*
*I had a **lovely** birthday.*

low lower, lowest
Something **low** is not very high.

lucky luckier, luckiest
If you are **lucky**, good things seem to happen to you.
*I'm really **lucky** – I've got a new bike!*

lump lumps
A **lump** is a solid piece of something.
*Mum put a few **lumps** of coal on the fire.*

lunch lunches
Lunch is the meal that you eat in the middle of the day.

lying See **lie**.

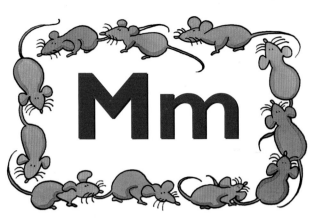

Mm

machine machines

A **machine** makes things or does a job. **Machines** often use electricity.
Our dirty clothes go into the washing machine.

made See **make**.

magazine magazines

A **magazine** is a thin book with lots of pictures. It usually comes out once a week or once a month.

magic

In fairy stories, **magic** things happen that could not happen in real life.
Cinderella's rags turned into a beautiful dress by magic!

magician magicians

A **magician** does clever tricks that seem impossible.
The magician pulled a rabbit out of an empty hat.

magnet magnets

A **magnet** is a special piece of metal that some metal things stick to.

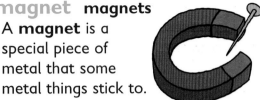

main

The **main** thing is the most important one.
The bank is on the main street.

make makes, making, made

1 When you **make** something, you put things together until you have something new.
We made a den out of boxes.
2 If you are **made** to do something, somebody sees that you do it.
My mum made me put my coat on.

male males

A **male** person or animal can be a father. Boys and men are **males**.

mammal mammals

A **mammal** is an animal that feeds its babies with its own milk. People, whales and cats are all **mammals**.

man men

A **man** is a grown-up male person.

a
b
c
d
e
f
g
h
i
j
k
l

Mm

n
o
p
q
r
s
t
u
v
w
x
y
z

manage **manages, managing, managed**
When you **manage** to do something, you are able to do something difficult.

many
Many means a lot of.
*There are **many** words in this dictionary.*

map **maps**
A **map** is a drawing that helps you find your way around.

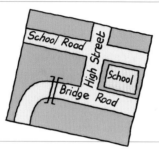

March
March is the third month of the year. It has 31 days.

mark **marks, marking, marked**
1 A **mark** is a spot or scratch that spoils something.
2 Your teacher gives you a **mark** for your work.
3 Your teacher **marks** your work to say whether it is right or wrong.

market **markets**
A **market** is a place where people buy and sell things.

marmalade
Marmalade is a kind of jam, usually made from oranges.

married
A **married** person has a husband or a wife.

marry **marries, marrying, married**
When two people **marry**, they become each other's husband and wife.

mask **masks**
You wear a **mask** over your face to make you look different.

mass
The **mass** of something is how much there is or how heavy it is.

mat **mats**
A **mat** is a thick piece of material. It protects a surface or makes it softer.

match **matches, matching, matched**
1 A **match** is a game between two teams.
2 A **match** is a little stick that people use to light a fire.
3 If you put similar things together, you **match** them.

material **materials**
1 **Material** is the stuff that things are made of. Metal, glass, wood and plastic are **materials**.
2 **Material** is also the cloth that is used to make things like clothes.

matter **matters, mattered**
If something **matters**, it is important.

mattress mattresses

A **mattress** is the thick, soft part of a bed that you sleep on.

may

1 If something **may** happen, it is possible that it will happen.
2 If someone says you **may** do something, you are allowed to do it.

May

May is the fifth month of the year. It has 31 days.

meal meals

You have a **meal** when you sit down and eat. Breakfast and dinner are both **meals**.

mean means, meaning, meant; meaner, meanest

1 If you know what something **means**, you are able to explain it.
*A dictionary explains what words **mean**.*
2 If you **mean** to do something, you plan to do it.
*I didn't **mean** to push you.*
3 A **mean** person is unkind and selfish.
*Don't be **mean** – share it with Ed!*

meanwhile

Meanwhile means while something else is happening.

measles

If you have **measles**, you have a fever and lots of red spots.

measure measures, measuring, measured

1 If you **measure** something, you find out its size. (See page 183.)

2 A **measure** is something you use when you **measure**, like a ruler or a jug.

meat

Meat is food that comes from part of an animal.

medicine medicines

When you are ill, you take **medicine** to make you better.

medium

Medium means neither large nor small.

meet meets, meeting, met

If you **meet** someone, you are in the same place at the same time.
*We will **meet** Sue at the station at midday.*

melon melons

A **melon** is a large, round, juicy fruit. It has yellow or green skin.

melt melts, melting, melted

When a solid **melts**, it changes into a liquid because it has been heated.
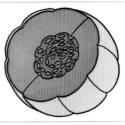
*The sun **melted** my lolly.*

a
b
c
d
e
f
g
h
i
j
k
l

Mm

n
o
p
q
r
s
t
u
v
w
x
y
z

memory **memories**
You use your **memory** when you remember things.
You learned that quickly – you have a good memory!

men See **man**.

mend **mends, mending, mended**
If you **mend** something that is broken, you put it right.
When I broke my radio, Mum mended it.

mental
Something **mental** is done in your head.
When you do mental maths, you work out the answer in your head.

menu **menus**
1 A **menu** in a restaurant is a list of what you can order to eat.
2 A **menu** on a computer screen is a list of things you can choose from.

mess
Things in a **mess** are untidy.

message **messages**
You send or leave a **message** when you cannot speak to someone yourself.
Dad left a message to say he'll be early.

messy **messier, messiest**
If something is **messy**, it is dirty or untidy.

met See **meet**.

metal **metals**
Metal is a hard, cold material. Steel is a **metal** used to make cars. Gold is a **metal** used to make jewellery.

method **methods**
A **method** is a way of doing something.

metre **metres**
You can measure length in **metres**. There are 100 centimetres (cm) in a **metre** (m).
John is 1 metre 50 centimetres tall.

mice See **mouse**.

microwave **microwaves**
A **microwave** oven cooks food very quickly.

midday
Midday means 12 o'clock in the middle of the day.

middle **middles**
The **middle** of something is between its edges or ends.
The cat is in the middle of the rug.

midnight
Midnight means 12 o'clock at night.

might
If something **might** happen, it is possible that it will.

mile   miles
A **mile** is a way to measure distance. A **mile** is longer than a kilometre.

milk
Milk is a white liquid. Female mammals make **milk** in their bodies to feed their babies. The **milk** that you drink comes from cows.

millennium   millennia
A **millennium** is 1000 years.

millilitre   millilitres
You can measure liquid in **millilitres**. There are 1000 **millilitres** (ml) in a litre (l).

millimetre   millimetres
You can measure length in **millimetres**. There are 10 **millimetres** (mm) in a centimetre (cm), and 1000 **millimetres** in a metre (m).

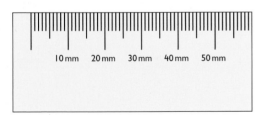

mind   minds, minding, minded
1 Your **mind** is your thoughts and memories.
2 If you **mind** about something, you care about it.
3 If you **mind** something for someone, you look after it.
*Could you **mind** my bag for a minute?*

mine
Mine means belonging to me.
*That pen is yours and this pen is **mine**.*

minus
Minus is another word you can use when you take away or subtract. The symbol − means **minus**.

minute   minutes
A **minute** is made up of 60 seconds. There are 60 **minutes** in an hour.

mirror   mirrors
A **mirror** is a special piece of glass. When you look in a **mirror**, you see yourself.

miss   misses, missing, missed
1 If you **miss** a bus or train, you arrive too late to catch it.
2 If you try to hit something and **miss**, you do not hit it.
3 If you **miss** someone, you feel sad because they are not with you.

Miss
Miss can be used before the name of a girl or unmarried woman.

missing
If something is **missing**, it is lost.

mistake   mistakes
A **mistake** is something that is wrong.
*Well done! You have made no **mistakes**.*

a
b
c
d
e
f
g
h
i
j
k
l
Mm
n
o
p
q
r
s
t
u
v
w
x
y
z

a
b
c
d
e
f
g
h
i
j
k
l

Mm

n
o
p
q
r
s
t
u
v
w
x
y
z

mix   mixes, mixing, mixed
When you **mix** things, you put them together to make something new.
Mix blue and yellow paint to make green.

mixture   mixtures
A **mixture** is a number of different things put together.
*This green paint is a **mixture** of blue and yellow.*

mobile phone   mobile phones
A **mobile phone** is a telephone that people can carry.

model   models
A **model** is a small copy of something. It shows what it looks like or how it works.
*Dan's building a **model** aeroplane.*

modern
If something is **modern**, it is new and uses the latest ideas and equipment.

mole   moles
1 A **mole** is a small, furry animal with tiny eyes. It lives under the ground.
2 A **mole** is also a small, dark spot on someone's skin.

moment   moments
A **moment** is a very short time.
*Jenny stopped for a **moment** to pull up her socks.*

Monday   Mondays
Monday is the day of the week between Sunday and Tuesday.

money
Money is the notes and coins you use to pay for things.

monkey   monkeys
A **monkey** is a small animal with a long tail. **Monkeys** live in hot countries and can climb trees.

monster   monsters
In stories, a **monster** is a huge, frightening creature.

month   months
A **month** has 28 to 31 days. There are 12 **months** in a year.

moon   moons
You see the **moon** shining in the sky at night. The **moon** moves around the Earth once every four weeks.

mop   mops
A **mop** is a long handle with strips of cloth joined to the end. You use a **mop** to wash the floor.

more
If someone has **more** than you, they have a larger number or amount than you have.

morning **mornings**
Morning is the first part of the day.
You get up in the **morning**.

mosque **mosques**
A **mosque** is a building where
people go to pray.

most
The person who has **most** has more
than anyone else.
*Richard has more books than me, but
Hirani has the most.*

moth **moths**
A **moth** is an insect that looks like a
butterfly. It usually flies around
at night.

mother **mothers**
A **mother** is a woman who has had
a child.

motorbike **motorbikes**
A **motorbike** is a vehicle with two
wheels and an engine.

motorway **motorways**
A **motorway** is a wide road. People
going a long way often use a
motorway.

mountain **mountains**
A **mountain** is a very high hill. It is
very steep and difficult to climb.
*Mount Everest is the highest mountain in
the world.*

mouse **mice**
1 A **mouse** is a small animal with a
long tail and sharp teeth.
2 You use a **mouse** to control the
pointer on a computer screen.

mouth **mouths**
You eat and speak with your **mouth**.
It is part of your face. (See page 174.)

move **moves, moving, moved**
If you **move**, you go to a different
place or position.

movement **movements**
When a person or thing moves, it
makes a **movement**.

Mr
Mr can be used before a man's name.

Mrs
Mrs can be used before the name of
a married woman.

Ms
Ms can be used before the name of
an unmarried or married woman.

much
Much means a lot.

mud
Mud is a wet and sticky mixture of
earth and water.

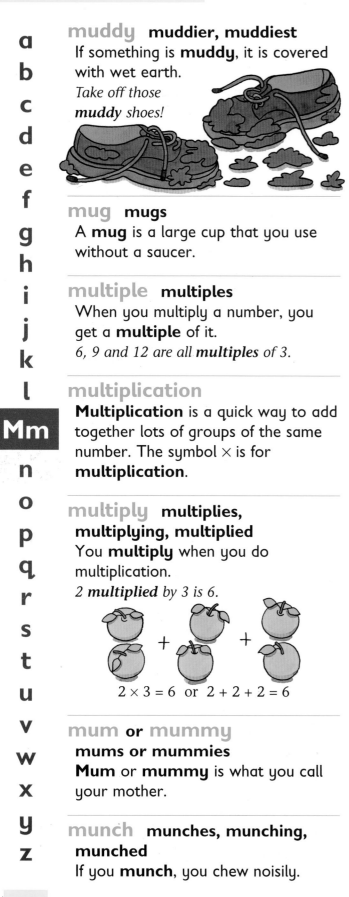

muddy **muddier, muddiest**

If something is **muddy**, it is covered with wet earth.

Take off those muddy shoes!

mug **mugs**

A **mug** is a large cup that you use without a saucer.

multiple **multiples**

When you multiply a number, you get a **multiple** of it.

6, 9 and 12 are all multiples of 3.

multiplication

Multiplication is a quick way to add together lots of groups of the same number. The symbol × is for **multiplication**.

multiply **multiplies, multiplying, multiplied**

You **multiply** when you do multiplication.

2 multiplied by 3 is 6.

$$2 × 3 = 6 \quad or \quad 2 + 2 + 2 = 6$$

mum or mummy **mums or mummies**

Mum or **mummy** is what you call your mother.

munch **munches, munching, munched**

If you **munch**, you chew noisily.

muscle **muscles**

Muscles are the parts inside your body that you use when you move.

You can feel a muscle in your arm when you bend it.

museum **museums**

You go to a **museum** to see lots of interesting things.

I saw a rocket at the Science Museum.

mushroom **mushrooms**

A **mushroom** is a plant with no leaves. You sometimes find **mushrooms** growing among grass.

music

Music is sounds made by people singing or playing instruments like pianos and recorders.

must

If someone **must** do something, they have to do it.

You must look before you cross the road!

my

My means belonging to me.

This is my bat and that is yours.

mystery **mysteries**

A **mystery** is something that people cannot explain or understand.

How my hamster escaped is a mystery!

Nn

nail **nails**

1 Your **nails** are the hard parts at the ends of your fingers and toes.

2 A **nail** is a piece of metal with a pointed end. It is used to join two pieces of wood together.

name **names**

A **name** is what you call a person, place or thing.

My name is Josie.

The name of France's capital city is Paris.

narrow **narrower, narrowest**

Something that is **narrow** measures very little between one side and the other.

nasty **nastier, nastiest**

Something **nasty** is not nice.

natural

Something that is **natural** is not made by people or machines.

Wood and cotton are natural materials, but plastic is not.

nature

Nature is everything in the world that is not made by people. Wild animals, mountains and the weather are part of **nature**.

naughty **naughtier, naughtiest**

A **naughty** child behaves badly.

near **nearer, nearest**

Something **near** is not far away.

nearly

Nearly means not quite.

Tara's nearly old enough to go to school. Harry nearly fell over.

neat **neater, neatest**

If something is **neat**, it is tidy. *Callum has folded his clothes into a neat pile.*

neck **necks**

Your **neck** joins your head to the rest of your body. (See page 174.)

necklace **necklaces**

A **necklace** is a piece of jewellery that is worn around the neck.

need **needs, needing, needed**

If you **need** something, you must have it.

I need a bag to carry my books.

needle **needles**

A **needle** is a thin piece of metal with a point. **Needles** are used for sewing. Special **needles** are used for knitting.

a
b
c
d
e
f
g
h
i
j
k
l
m
Nn
o
p
q
r
s
t
u
v
w
x
y
z

a
b
c
d
e
f
g
h
i
j
k
l
m

Nn

o
p
q
r
s
t
u
v
w
x
y
z

neighbour neighbours

A **neighbour** is someone who lives very near you.

nephew nephews

A person's **nephew** is the son of their brother or sister.

nervous

If you are **nervous**, you feel worried or afraid.

nest nests

A **nest** is the home that some animals make for their young ones.

net nets

1 Net is a material with lots of holes. It is made of knotted thread or string.
2 A **net** is used to catch fish, or in some games like tennis and football.
The ball shot into the back of the net.

nettle nettles

A **nettle** is a wild plant. It has rough leaves that sting.

never

If something **never** happens, it does not happen at any time.
Greg never gets to school on time.

new newer, newest

1 Something **new** has not been used before.
2 New also means different.
We did something new today – we played rounders.

news

News is information about things that have just happened.
I've got some exciting news! I won my race!

newspaper newspapers

A **newspaper** tells you in words and pictures what has happened in the world.

next

1 Next means the one nearest to you.
I spoke to the girl at the next table.
2 Next also means the one that comes after this one.
I'll see you next week.

nice nicer, nicest

If something or someone is **nice**, you like them.

niece nieces

A person's **niece** is the daughter of their brother or sister.

night nights

Night is the time when it is dark and most people sleep.
Did you see the stars last night?

nightdress nightdresses
A **nightdress** is a loose dress that girls and women wear in bed. (See page 176.)

nightmare nightmares
A **nightmare** is a frightening dream.

no
1 If you say **no**, you do not agree with someone or you will not do something.
2 No also means none at all.
*My uncle has **no** children.*

nobody
Nobody means no person or no one.
*I opened the door but **nobody** was there.*

nod nods, nodding, nodded
When you **nod**, you move your head up and down quickly.

noise noises
Noise is the sounds that someone or something makes.
*The **noise** of the storm kept me awake.*

noisy noisier, noisiest
Something **noisy** makes a lot of noise.

none
None means not one.
*Sunil has 12 pencils but I have **none**.*

non-fiction
Non-fiction books tell you about real people and things.

nonsense
If someone talks **nonsense**, what they say does not mean anything.

noon
Noon means 12 o'clock in the middle of the day.

no one or no-one
No one means not one person or nobody.
*I opened the door but **no one** was there.*

north
North is a direction. It is on your left when you look towards the rising sun in the morning.

nose noses
Your **nose** is part of your face. You breathe and smell through your **nose**. (See page 174.)

nostril nostrils
Your **nostrils** are the two holes in your nose that you breathe through.

a
b
c
d
e
f
g
h
i
j
k
l
m
Nn
o
p
q
r
s
t
u
v
w
x
y
z

a
b
c
d
e
f
g
h
i
j
k
l
m
Nn
o
p
q
r
s
t
u
v
w
x
y
z

note   notes
1 A **note** is a short letter.
2 You make **notes** to help you remember something.
3 A **note** is also a piece of paper money.
4 A **note** can also be a single sound in music.

nothing
If you do not have anything, you have **nothing**.

notice   notices, noticing, noticed
1 If you **notice** something, you see it and start to think about it.
2 A **notice** is a sign that tells people something.
*The **notice** said: "Keep off the grass".*

Keep off the grass

noun   nouns
A **noun** is a word for a person, animal, place or thing.

November
November is the eleventh month of the year. It has 30 days.

now
Now means at the present time.
*You are reading these words **now**.*

nowhere
Nowhere means not any place.
*We have **nowhere** to play football when the park is closed.*

number   numbers
A **number** can be written using letters or symbols. You use **numbers** to count things or people.
*You can see more **numbers** on page 183.*

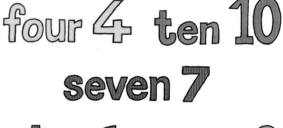

3 three   **four 4**   **ten 10**
seven 7
six 6   **two 2**

nurse   nurses
A **nurse** looks after ill people.
Nurses usually work in hospitals.

nursery   nurseries
1 A **nursery** is a place where young children go to play and learn.
2 A **nursery** school is a school for children from three to five years old.

nursery rhyme
nursery rhymes
A **nursery rhyme** is a poem or song for young children.

nut   nuts
A **nut** is a dry brown seed inside a hard shell. It grows on a tree.

Oo

oak oaks
An **oak** is a large tree. It has seeds called acorns. Its hard wood is often used to make furniture.

oar oars
An **oar** is a long pole with a flat end. You pull on an **oar** to move a boat through water.

oats
Oats are the seeds of a plant. They are used to make food for people and animals.

obey obeys, obeying, obeyed
When you **obey** someone, you do what they say.

ocean oceans
An **ocean** is a huge sea.

o'clock
You use **o'clock** when you say a time that is exactly on the hour.
*Five **o'clock** means exactly five hours after noon or midnight.*

octagon octagons
An **octagon** is a flat shape that has eight sides. (See page 184.)

October
October is the tenth month of the year. It has 31 days.

octopus octopuses
An **octopus** is a sea creature. It catches food with its eight long arms.

odd odder, oddest
1 An **odd** number cannot be divided exactly by two. There will always be one left over.
2 Something **odd** is a bit strange.

off
1 If you take **off** your coat, you do not wear it any more.
2 If a light or machine is **off**, it is not switched on.
3 When you get **off** something, you are not on it any more.
*We get **off** the bus at the next stop.*

offer offers, offering, offered
If you **offer** something to someone, you ask if they would like it.
*I **offered** Ronan some ice cream.*

office offices
An **office** is a room where people work.

often
Often means many times.
*We **often** have a picnic outside in the summer.*

a
b
c
d
e
f
g
h
i
j
k
l
m
n

Oo

p
q
r
s
t
u
v
w
x
y
z

oil oils

Oil is a smooth, thick liquid. One kind of **oil** is burned to keep people warm or used in machines. Another kind of **oil** is used for cooking food.

old older, oldest

An **old** person was born a long time ago. Something **old** was made a long time ago.

once

1 If something happens **once**, it happens one time only.
2 If something happens at **once**, it happens straight away.

onion onions

An **onion** is a white vegetable with a strong taste.

only

Only means one or no more than.
*You can **only** have one chocolate.*
*Gary's little – he's **only** three.*
*This is the **only** box I can find.*

open opens, opening, opened

1 When something is **open**, it is no longer closed.
2 If you **open** something, you make it **open**.
*Dad **opened** the door.*

operation operations

When doctors repair a person's body, they do an **operation**.

opposite opposites

The **opposite** of something is different from it in every way.
*Light is the **opposite** of dark.*

orange oranges

1 An **orange** is a round, juicy fruit. It has a thick **orange** skin.

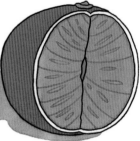

2 **Orange** is a colour made from a mixture of red and yellow. (See page 184.)

orchestra orchestras

An **orchestra** is a large group of people who play musical instruments together.

order orders, ordering, ordered

1 The **order** of things is how they are arranged.
The words in this book are in alphabetical order.
2 If you **order** something in a restaurant, you say you would like it.
3 If you are **ordered** to do something, you must do it.

ordinary

Ordinary means not special in any way.

*It was a very **ordinary** day. Nothing different happened.*

other

Other means not this one.

*Take your bag in this hand and hold the rail with the **other**.*

otter **otters**

An **otter** is a furry long-tailed animal. It lives near water. **Otters** swim well and eat fish.

our

Our means belonging to us.

*This is **our** car.*

out

1 If you go **out**, you are away from home.

*We went **out** for a meal.*

2 If a light or fire goes **out**, it stops burning.

outside

1 The **outside** of something is the part around the rest of it.

2 If you are **outside**, you are not in a building.

oval **ovals**

An **oval** is a flat shape with a curved edge. It is like the shape of an egg.

oven **ovens**

An **oven** is the cupboard in a cooker where you bake food.

over

When something is **over**, it is finished.

*When the game was **over** we all went home.*

owe **owes, owing, owed**

If you **owe** someone money, you have not paid them for something or you have not paid back what they lent you.

owl **owls**

An **owl** is a bird that usually hunts at night. It has large eyes to help it to see in the dark.

own **owns, owning, owned**

1 If you **own** something, it belongs to you.

2 If you are on your **own**, you are alone.

a
b
c
d
e
f
g
h
i
j
k
l
m
n
Oo
p
q
r
s
t
u
v
w
x
y
z

a b c d e f g h i j k l m n o **Pp** q r s t u v w x y z

pack   packs, packing, packed

When you **pack** a case or container, you put things in it.

*Masud **packed** his bags and went on holiday.*

packet   packets

A **packet** is a small container made of paper or cardboard. Breakfast cereals and sugar come in **packets**.

paddle   paddles, paddling, paddled

When you **paddle**, you walk in water which is not very deep.

page   pages

A **page** is one side of a piece of paper in a book, magazine or newspaper.

*This is **page** 104 of this dictionary.*

paid   See **pay**.

pain   pains

You feel a **pain** when part of your body hurts.

paint   paints, painting, painted

1 **Paint** is a liquid that you use to change the colour of something.
2 You can **paint** walls or pictures.

painting   paintings

A **painting** is a picture that someone has painted.

pair   pairs

1 Two things that go together make a **pair**. Shoes, feet and eyes all come in **pairs**.
2 Something that has two similar parts joined together can also be a **pair**.

*I want a **pair** of shoes to go with this **pair** of trousers.*

palace   palaces

A **palace** is a very large house. Kings, queens and other important people live in **palaces**.

pale   paler, palest

If a colour is **pale**, it is almost white.

palm   palms

1 Your **palm** is the inside part of your hand. (See page 174.)

2 A **palm** tree grows in hot countries. It has large leaves but no branches.

pan **pans**
A **pan** is a round, metal container with a long handle. It is used for cooking things on top of a cooker.

pancake **pancakes**
A **pancake** is a very thin, flat cake. It is cooked in a flat pan.

panda **pandas**
A **panda** is a large black and white animal. It looks like a bear and lives in China.

panic **panics, panicking, panicked**
1 **Panic** is a sudden feeling of fear.
2 If you **panic**, you feel so afraid that you cannot think properly.

pantomime **pantomimes**
A **pantomime** is a kind of play that children see at Christmas time. It tells a fairy story and has songs and jokes.

pants
You wear **pants** under your trousers or skirt.

paper **papers**
1 **Paper** is a thin material. You write on **paper** and wrap parcels with it. Books are printed on **paper**.
2 **Paper** is also short for newspaper.

parcel **parcels**
You wrap something in a **parcel** to send it in the post or give it as a present.

parent **parents**
Your **parents** are your mother and your father.

park **parks, parking, parked**
1 A **park** is a large open space with grass and trees. People walk and play in **parks**.
2 When someone **parks** a car, they leave it for a short time.

parrot **parrots**
A **parrot** is a brightly coloured bird with a curved beak. Some **parrots** copy human speech.

part **parts**
A **part** is anything that belongs to something bigger.
*Your eyes, nose and mouth are **parts** of your face.*

party **parties**
A **party** is a group of people having fun together.

pass **passes, passing, passed**
1 When you **pass** something, you go by it without stopping.
2 When you **pass** something to someone, you give it to them.
3 If you **pass** a test, you do well.

a
b
c
d
e
f
g
h
i
j
k
l
m
n
o
Pp
q
r
s
t
u
v
w
x
y
z

a
b
c
d
e
f
g
h
i
j
k
l
m
n
o

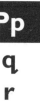

Pp

q
r
s
t
u
v
w
x
y
z

passenger **passengers**
A **passenger** travels in a car, bus, train, aeroplane or ship.

passport **passports**
A **passport** is a small book that you carry when you travel to another country.

past
The **past** is the time before now.
*One minute ago, ten years ago and thousands of years ago are all in the **past**.*

pasta
Pasta is a food that you eat with sauce. Spaghetti, macaroni and noodles are all different types of **pasta**.

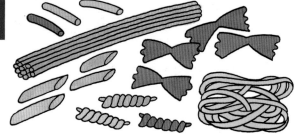

paste **pastes, pasting, pasted**
1 **Paste** is a kind of glue. It is used for sticking paper onto things.
2 If you **paste** something, you stick it with glue or **paste**.

pastry
Pastry is a mixture of flour, fat and water. It is rolled flat and baked. Tarts and pies are made with **pastry**.

pat **pats, patting, patted**
When you **pat** something, you touch it gently with the palm of your hand.
*Carlos **patted** the dog on the head.*

path **paths**
A **path** is like a small lane for people to walk along.
*We took the **path** through the forest.*

patient **patients**
1 A **patient** is an ill person who is being looked after.
2 A **patient** person stays calm when things go wrong.
*Please be **patient** – dinner's a bit late today.*

pattern **patterns**
1 A **pattern** is a set of repeated marks.

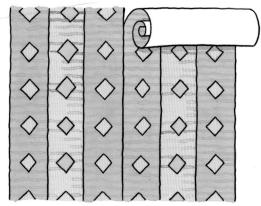

2 A **pattern** is also the way that numbers or letters are related to one another.
*Find the **pattern** in these numbers: 2, 4, 6, 8.*

pavement **pavements**
A **pavement** is a hard path at the side of a road.
*Don't walk in the road! Stay on the **pavement**.*

paw **paws**
A **paw** is the foot of an animal such as a cat or a bear.

pay **pays, paying, paid**
If you **pay** for something, you give money for it.

PC **PCs**
A **PC** is a computer that is used by one or two people at a time. **PC** is short for personal computer.

pea **peas**
A **pea** is a small, round, green vegetable. **Peas** grow in long, green shells called pods.

peace
Peace is a quiet time, when no one is fighting.

peach **peaches**
A **peach** is a round, soft, juicy fruit. It has a large stone and a furry skin.

peacock **peacocks**
A **peacock** is a large, blue and green male bird. It can open its tail like a fan. The female is called a peahen.

peanut **peanuts**
A **peanut** is a small nut. It grows in a shell under the ground.

pear **pears**
A **pear** is a juicy fruit that grows on a tree.

pebble **pebbles**
A **pebble** is a small, round stone.

peck **pecks, pecking, pecked**
When a bird **pecks**, it bites at something quickly with its beak.

pedal **pedals, pedalling, pedalled**
1 A **pedal** is part of a bike. (See page 175.)
2 When you **pedal** a bike, you push the **pedals** with your feet.

peel **peels, peeling, peeled**
1 **Peel** is the skin of some fruit and vegetables.
2 When you **peel** something, you take off its skin.

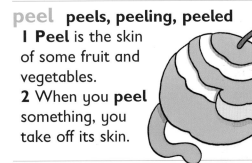

peg **pegs**
You use a **peg** when you hang something up.
*Mum uses clothes **pegs** to hang the washing on the line.*

pen **pens**
You use a **pen** when you write or draw with ink.
*I drew this picture with a **pen**.*

pence See **penny**.

pencil **pencils**
A **pencil** is a thin stick of wood with a grey or coloured centre. You use a **pencil** to write or draw.

a
b
c
d
e
f
g
h
i
j
k
l
m
n
o
Pp
q
r
s
t
u
v
w
x
y
z

a
b
c
d
e
f
g
h
i
j
k
l
m
n
o

Pp

q
r
s
t
u
v
w
x
y
z

penguin penguins

A **penguin** is a large black and white bird that lives where it is very cold. It cannot fly but uses its wings for swimming.

penny pence or pennies

A **penny** is a British coin.
There are 100 **pence** in a pound.
The symbol for **pence** is p.

pentagon pentagons

A **pentagon** is a flat shape that has five sides. (See page 184.)

people

People means more than one person. See **person**.

pepper peppers

1 Pepper is a powder with a hot taste used to flavour food.
2 A **pepper** is a hollow red, green or yellow vegetable. It sometimes tastes hot and spicy.

perform performs, performing, performed

1 When you **perform**, you do something in front of an audience.
*The magician **performed** his magic tricks on the stage.*
2 When you **perform** an action, you do it.

period periods

A **period** of time has a beginning and an end.
*The rain fell for short **periods** of time.*

person people

A **person** is a man, woman or child.
A **person** can also be called a human.

pest pests

A **pest** is an insect or small animal that damages plants and crops.

pet pets

A **pet** is an animal that you look after. **Pets** often live in your home.
*We keep a dog, a cat and a pony as **pets**.*

petal petals

A **petal** is a coloured part of a flower.

petrol

People put **petrol** in a car to make the engine work.

phone phones

You use a **phone** to speak to someone in another place. **Phone** is short for telephone.

photograph photographs, photographing, photographed

1 A **photograph,** or **photo**, is a picture made using a camera and film.
2 If you **photograph** something, you take a **photo** of it.

piano pianos
A **piano** is a large musical instrument. You press black and white keys to make music.

pick picks, picking, picked
1 When you **pick** something, you choose it.
2 If you **pick** a flower, you take it off its plant.
3 When you **pick** something up, you lift it.

picnic picnics
If you have a **picnic**, you carry a meal somewhere and eat it outside.
*We took a **picnic** to the beach.*

pictogram pictograms
A **pictogram** is a kind of graph. It uses pictures instead of lines.

 = 1 child

picture pictures
A **picture** is a drawing, painting or photograph.

pie pies
A **pie** is fruit, meat or other food covered in pastry and baked in the oven.

piece pieces
A **piece** of something is a part of it.
*Mum gave me a **piece** of apple pie.*

pier piers
A **pier** is a long platform built out into the sea.

pig pigs
A **pig** is a farm animal. It has a snout and a curly tail. The meat from a **pig** is called pork.

pigeon pigeons
A **pigeon** is a bird that is often seen in towns and cities.

pile piles
A **pile** is a number of things put on top of one another.
*Please put your clothes in a neat **pile**.*

pill pills
A **pill** is a kind of medicine. It is small and round so that it can be swallowed without chewing.

pillow pillows
A **pillow** is a bag filled with soft material. You rest your head on a **pillow** when you are in bed.

pilot pilots
A **pilot** flies an aeroplane.

a
b
c
d
e
f
g
h
i
j
k
l
m
n
o
Pp
q
r
s
t
u
v
w
x
y
z

109

a
b
c
d
e
f
g
h
i
j
k
l
m
n
o

Pp

q
r
s
t
u
v
w
x
y
z

pin **pins**
A **pin** is a short, thin piece of metal with a sharp point. You use **pins** to hold pieces of cloth together.

pineapple **pineapples**
A **pineapple** is a large fruit with sweet, juicy yellow flesh. It has a thick, lumpy brown skin and grows in hot countries.

pint **pints**
Liquids like milk can be measured in **pints**.

pipe **pipes**
A **pipe** is a long tube. **Pipes** carry liquids or gas from one place to another.

pirate **pirates**
A **pirate** is a sailor who attacks and robs other ships.

pizza **pizzas**
A **pizza** is a round, flat piece of bread covered with cheese, tomatoes and other foods. It is baked in a very hot oven.

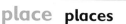

place **places**
1 A **place** is a piece of land or a building.
2 A **place** is where something or someone is.
*Don't move – stay in your **places**!*
3 The number 542 has a 5 in the hundreds **place**, a 4 in the tens **place** and a 2 in the units **place**.

plain **plainer, plainest**
Plain means simple or without decoration.
*Emma wore a **plain** green top.*

plan **plans, planning, planned**
1 If you **plan** something, you decide how to do it.
2 A **plan** is a drawing or diagram of something that is to be made.

plane **planes**
A **plane** is a large flying vehicle that carries people or things. It has wings and one or more engines. **Plane** is short for aeroplane.

planet **planets**
A **planet** is a large, round object in space that moves around a star. Earth is a **planet** that travels around the Sun once a year. Some **planets** have rings.

plant **plants, planting, planted**
1 A **plant** is anything that lives that is not an animal. Trees and flowers are **plants**. Mushrooms and grass are **plants**, too.
2 If you **plant** something, you put seeds or **plants** into the ground to grow.
*We've **planted** some poppy seeds in the garden.*

plaster **plasters**

1 A **plaster** is a strip of material that you stick on when you cut yourself.

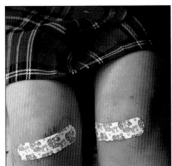

2 Plaster is also a soft, white mixture that goes hard when it dries. **Plaster** is spread on walls to make them smooth.

plastic **plastics**

Plastic is a strong, light material made in factories. It is used for buckets, bottles, plates, toys and many other things.

plate **plates**

A **plate** is a flat dish that you put food on.

platform **platforms**

1 You stand on a **platform** so that you can be seen easily. It is higher than the rest of the room.
2 You stand on a **platform** at a railway station to wait for a train.

play **plays, playing, played**

1 When you **play** a game, you do something for fun.
2 If you **play** a musical instrument, you make music with it.
3 A **play** is a story that is performed by actors.

playground **playgrounds**

A **playground** is a place outside where children play.

playtime

Playtime is when you come out of the classroom to play.

please **pleases, pleasing, pleased**

1 If you **please** someone, you make them happy.
2 You say **please** when you ask for something.
Please may I have an ice cream?

plenty

If there is **plenty** of something, there is a lot of it.
*Help yourself – there's **plenty** of food!*

plough **ploughs**

A **plough** is a farm tool. It cuts up the earth so that seeds can be planted.

plum **plums**

A **plum** is a small, juicy red or yellow fruit. It has a smooth skin and a stone in the middle.

plump **plumper, plumpest**

If someone or something is **plump**, they are a bit fat.
*Our cat is **plump** and cuddly.*

plural **plurals**

Plural means more than one. Many **plural** words end in the letter s.
*"Dogs" is the **plural** of "dog".*
*"Children" is the **plural** of "child".*

a
b
c
d
e
f
g
h
i
j
k
l
m
n
o
Pp
q
r
s
t
u
v
w
x
y
z

a
b
c
d
e
f
g
h
i
j
k
l
m
n
o

Pp

q
r
s
t
u
v
w
x
y
z

plus

Plus is another word you can use when you add. The symbol + means **plus**.

pocket pockets

A **pocket** is a small bag sewn into clothes. You keep things in your **pockets**.

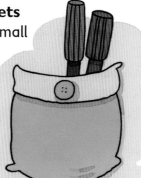

poem poems

A **poem** is a piece of writing that uses language in a special way. It uses rhythm and often rhyme.

poet poets

A **poet** is a person who writes poems.

poetry

Poetry means poems or a collection of poems.

point points, pointing, pointed

1 If you **point** at something, you hold your finger towards it to show where it is.
2 The **point** of something is the sharp part at the end.

pointed

Something **pointed** has a sharp point at the end.

poisonous

If something is **poisonous**, it makes you ill if you eat or drink it.
*Some mushrooms are **poisonous**.*

polar bear polar bears

A **polar bear** is a large white bear. It lives near the North Pole.

pole poles

1 A **pole** is a long, thin piece of wood or metal.
*The tent was held up by metal **poles**.*
2 The North **Pole** and the South **Pole** are places at opposite ends of the Earth.
*The **Poles** are covered in ice and are the coldest places on Earth.*

police

The **police** are men and women who make sure that no one breaks the law. They are often called **policemen**, **policewomen** or **police officers**.
*The **police** are looking for the burglars.*

polish polishes, polishing, polished

If you **polish** something, you rub it to make it shine. You often use a cloth with **polish** on it.

polite

A **polite** person behaves well and is not rude.
*It is **polite** to hold the door open for other people.*

pond ponds

A **pond** is a small area of water in a garden or field.

pony ponies
A **pony** is a small horse.

pool pools
1 A **pool** is a small area of still water next to the sea.
Paul and Martha found lots of little crabs in the rock pool.
2 Pool is also short for swimming **pool**.

poor poorer, poorest
A **poor** person does not have very much money.

pop pops, popping, popped
1 If you **pop** a balloon, it bursts with a short, sharp sound.
2 Pop is modern popular music.

popcorn
You eat **popcorn** as a snack with salt or sugar. Seeds of corn are heated until they burst.

poppy poppies
A **poppy** is a wild plant. It has a large red flower.

popular
If something is **popular**, lots of people like it.

porridge
Porridge is a hot breakfast cereal. It is made from oats and water or milk.

position positions
1 Your **position** is where you are or how your body is arranged.
2 Your **position** is also where you play in a team.
"What position do you play?" "I'm the goalkeeper."

possible
If something is **possible**, it can be done or can happen.
It's still possible to get tickets for the match.

post posts, posting, posted
1 The **post** is the letters that come to your house.

2 When you **post** a letter, you put it in a postbox.
3 A **post** is a piece of wood or metal fixed upright in the ground.

poster posters
A **poster** is a large notice or picture. It is put up to tell people about something.
Did you see the poster on the wall about the pantomime?

postman postmen
A **postman** collects and delivers letters and parcels.

a
b
c
d
e
f
g
h
i
j
k
l
m
n
o
Pp
q
r
s
t
u
v
w
x
y
z

a
b
c
d
e
f
g
h
i
j
k
l
m
n
o

Pp

q
r
s
t
u
v
w
x
y
z

post office   post offices

A **post office** is a shop where you can send letters and parcels. It also sells stamps.

pot   pots

A **pot** is a round container. **Pots** hold many different things, and some are used for cooking food.

potato   potatoes

A **potato** is a common vegetable. It grows under the ground. Chips and crisps are made from **potatoes**.

pound   pounds

British money is measured in **pounds** and pence. The symbol for **pound** is £.

pour   pours, pouring, poured

1 If you **pour** a liquid, you tip it out of its container.
2 When it is **pouring** with rain, it is raining heavily.

powder

Powder is a solid material that is in very tiny pieces. Flour is a **powder**.

power

The **power** of something is its strength.
*A lorry's engine has more **power** than a car's engine.*

practice   practices

Practice means doing something many times to get better at it.
*Try to get lots of spelling **practice** before the test.*

practise   practises, practising, practised

If you **practise** something, you do it many times to get better at it.
*I am **practising** my song for the show.*

pram   prams

You can push a baby from place to place in a **pram**.

pray   prays, praying, prayed

If you **pray**, you talk to your god.

predict   predicts, predicting, predicted

If you **predict** something, you say it will happen in the future.

present   presents

1 You give people **presents** on their birthday or at Christmas.
2 The **present** is now.
3 If you are **present** somewhere, you are there.

press   presses, pressing, pressed

When you **press** something, you push hard on it.
*Mick **pressed** the doorbell.*

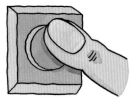

pretend **pretends, pretending, pretended**
If you **pretend**, you try to be something you are not.
*Let's **pretend** to be pirates. This tree can be our ship.*

pretty **prettier, prettiest**
Pretty means nice to look at.
*Those kittens are really **pretty**!*

price **prices**
The **price** of something is the money you pay for it.

prick **pricks, pricking, pricked**
If you **prick** something, you make a tiny hole using a sharp point.

prince **princes**
A **prince** is the son of a king or queen.

princess **princesses**
1 The daughter of a king or queen is called a **princess**.
2 The wife of a prince is sometimes called a **princess**.

print **prints, printing, printed**
When words and pictures are **printed**, they are put on the paper using a machine. Usually lots of copies are **printed** at once.
*The pages of this dictionary are **printed**.*

printer **printers**
1 A **printer** prints books or newspapers using a machine.
2 A **printer** is also a machine that prints information from a computer.

prison **prisons**
People who have broken the law sometimes go to **prison**.

prize **prizes**
You win a **prize** if you are very good at something or by being lucky.

problem **problems**
A **problem** is something that is hard to sort out.
*I've got a **problem** – my lace is broken.*

program **programs**
A **program** is a set of instructions that tell a computer what to do.

programme **programmes**
1 A **programme** is a show on television or radio.
2 A **programme** is a small book of information about a show or a sports match.

project **projects**
If you are doing a **project**, you find lots of information about something and then write about it.
*I did a **project** on dinosaurs at school.*

a
b
c
d
e
f
g
h
i
j
k
l
m
n
o
Pp
q
r
s
t
u
v
w
x
y
z

a
b
c
d
e
f
g
h
i
j
k
l
m
n
o

Pp

q
r
s
t
u
v
w
x
y
z

promise promises, promising, promised

If you **promise** to do something, you mean that you really will do it.
*Mum **promised** that we'd go to the swings today.*

pronoun pronouns

A **pronoun** is a word like "me" or "your". It is used instead of a noun. (See page 179.)

proper

Proper means right or correct.
*Put those books back in their **proper** place, please.*

protect protects, protecting, protected

If you **protect** someone or something, you keep them safe.
*Ruby wore a helmet to **protect** her head when she rode her bike.*

proud prouder, proudest

When you are **proud** of someone, you feel very pleased with them because they have done well.
*This school is very **proud** of the winning netball team.*

prove proves, proving, proved

When you **prove** something, you show that it is true.
*I can **prove** Neil wasn't there because he was at my house!*

publisher publishers

A **publisher** prints and sells books, newspapers or magazines.

pudding puddings

A **pudding** is a sweet food that you eat at the end of a meal.

puddle puddles

A **puddle** is a small pool of water that is left after rain.

pull pulls, pulling, pulled

When you **pull** something, you hold it and make it come towards you.

pumpkin pumpkins

A **pumpkin** is a large, round, orange vegetable. People make **pumpkin** lanterns at Halloween.

punctuation

Punctuation means signs like full stops, commas and question marks. Here are some **punctuation** marks:
. , " " ' ! ?

puncture punctures

A **puncture** is a small hole made by something sharp. If a tyre has a **puncture**, the air gets out and it goes flat.
*Dad mended the **puncture** in my tyre.*

punish   punishes, punishing, punished

If someone is **punished**, they are made unhappy because they have done something wrong.

*Mum **punished** Jenny for being rude by sending her to her room.*

punishment   punishments

A **punishment** is something unpleasant that happens to someone who has done wrong.

pupil   pupils

1 The **pupils** at school are the children who go there to learn.
2 The **pupil** of your eye is the black part in the middle.

puppet   puppets

A **puppet** is a small toy figure of a person or animal. You move a **puppet** by pulling strings or by putting your hand inside its body.

puppy   puppies

A **puppy** is a young dog.

pure   purer, purest

Something that is **pure** has nothing else mixed with it.

purse   purses

You keep money in a **purse**.

push   pushes, pushing, pushed

If you **push** something, you move it away from you with your hands.

pushchair   pushchairs

A **pushchair** is a small folding chair on wheels. Little children are taken around in **pushchairs**.

put   puts, putting, put

When you **put** something somewhere, you place it there.

*I **put** my book in my bag.*

puzzle   puzzles

A **puzzle** is something that is hard to understand or work out. People do **puzzles** for fun.

*I enjoyed doing the crossword **puzzle**.*

pyjamas

Pyjamas are a loose top and trousers that you wear in bed.

pyramid   pyramids

1 A **pyramid** is a solid shape. Its sides are triangles that meet in a point at the top.
2 The **Pyramids** are huge stone buildings in Egypt.

a
b
c
d
e
f
g
h
i
j
k
l
m
n
o
Pp
q
r
s
t
u
v
w
x
y
z

a
b
c
d
e
f
g
h
i
j
k
l
m
n
o
p
Qq
r
s
t
u
v
w
x
y
z

quack quacks

A **quack** is the cry of a duck. It is a loud, hard sound.

quarrel quarrels, quarrelling, quarrelled

1 A **quarrel** is an angry argument.
2 When you **quarrel** with someone, you talk angrily to each other.
My sister and I quarrelled about who should clean out the rabbit hutch.

quarter quarters

1 When you divide something exactly into four, each piece is a **quarter**.

$\frac{1}{4}$

2 Quarter past ten means 15 minutes after ten o'clock. **Quarter** to ten means 15 minutes before ten o'clock.

queen queens

1 A **queen** is a woman who rules a country because she belongs to a royal family.
2 The wife of a king is also called a **queen**.

question questions

When you ask a **question**, you want to know something.
Who can answer Alice's question about the homework?

question mark question marks

A **question mark** is used at the end of a sentence that asks a question.
Does this sentence need a question mark? Is it asking a question?

queue queues

When you are in a **queue**, you are standing in a line of people waiting for something.
There was a queue outside the cinema.

quick quicker, quickest

Something **quick** does not take long.
Can I have a quick look at your book?

quickly

If you do something **quickly**, you do it in very little time.

quiet quieter, quietest

When someone is **quiet**, they make very little noise.

quite

1 Quite means more than a bit.
I am quite hungry but not starving.
2 Not **quite** means nearly.
I have not quite finished my writing.

quiz quizzes

A **quiz** is a kind of game. People are asked questions to find out who knows most.

Rr

rabbit   rabbits
A **rabbit** is a small furry animal with long ears. Wild **rabbits** live in tunnels under the ground.

race   races
A **race** is a competition to see who is the fastest.
My friend won the sack race.

radiator   radiators
A **radiator** is a metal container filled with liquid. It is used to heat a room.

radio   radios
A **radio** turns waves in the air into programmes that you can hear.
I listen to music on my radio.

raft   rafts
A **raft** is a flat boat. It is made from long pieces of wood joined together.

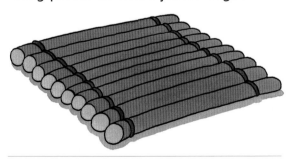

rag   rags
A **rag** is a piece of old cloth. **Rags** are used to clean or wipe things.

railway   railways
A **railway** is the metal bars that trains run along.

rain   rains, raining, rained
When it **rains**, little drops of water called **rain** fall from the sky.

rainbow   rainbows
A **rainbow** is a band of different colours in the sky. You sometimes see a **rainbow** when the sun shines through rain. The colours of the **rainbow** are red, orange, yellow, green, blue, indigo and violet.

raise   raises, raising, raised
1 If you **raise** something, you lift it up higher.
2 If you **raise** your voice, you speak louder.

rake   rakes
A **rake** is a garden tool used for collecting leaves and grass into piles. It has a row of metal teeth and a long handle.

Ramadan
Ramadan is a time when Muslims do not eat or drink during daylight hours.

ran   See **run**.

a
b
c
d
e
f
g
h
i
j
k
l
m
n
o
p
q
Rr
s
t
u
v
w
x
y
z

rang See **ring**.

rare **rarer, rarest**
Something that is **rare** is not seen very often.
*This is a **rare** bird – there are only fifty in the whole world.*

raspberry **raspberries**
A **raspberry** is a small, soft, red fruit.

rat **rats**
A **rat** is an animal that looks like a large mouse. It has sharp teeth and a long tail.

rather
1 If you would **rather** do something, you would like to do it more than something else.
*I'd **rather** stay in than go out.*
2 If something is **rather** cold, it is a bit cold.

rattle **rattles, rattling, rattled**
1 When something **rattles**, it makes short, quick, knocking sounds.
2 A **rattle** is a toy which a baby shakes to make a noise.

raw
Raw food is not cooked.
Raw carrots are sweet and crisp.

reach **reaches, reaching, reached**
1 When you **reach** a place, you arrive there.
2 When you **reach** for something, you stretch out your hand towards it.
*I **reached** for a book on the top shelf.*

read **reads, reading, read**
1 When you can turn written letters into words and sentences, you can **read**.
2 When you **read** aloud, you say the words that are written.
*I am **reading** a bedtime story.*

ready
If you are **ready**, you can start straight away.
*I've packed my bag and I'm **ready** to go.*

real
1 If something is **real**, it is a fact or it is true.
*This is a story about a **real** person who is still alive today.*
2 A **real** thing is exactly what it is meant to be and not a copy.
*This is a **real** diamond, not a piece of glass.*

really
You use **really** to show that something is true.
*Did you **really** see a monkey at the zoo?*
*I'm **really** tired.*

rearrange **rearranges, rearranging, rearranged**
If you **rearrange** things, you put them in a different order.

reason **reasons**
A **reason** tells you why something has happened.
*The **reason** I'm late is that the bus broke down.*

receive **receives, receiving, received**
If you **receive** something, it is sent or given to you.
*I **received** a letter from my granny.*

recipe **recipes**
A **recipe** is a set of instructions. It tells you how to make something to eat or drink.

recite **recites, reciting, recited**
If you **recite** a poem, you say it out loud.

record **records, recording, recorded**
1 Someone who does something better than anybody else sets a **record**.
2 If you **record** something, you put it on tape or write it down.

recorder **recorders**
A **recorder** is a musical instrument. It is played by blowing into one end.

recount **recounts, recounting, recounted**
If you **recount** a story, you tell it.

rectangle **rectangles**
A **rectangle** is a shape with four sides and four corners that are all right angles. Its opposite sides are the same length.

rectangular
Anything in the shape of a rectangle is **rectangular**. A football pitch is **rectangular**.

reflection **reflections**
1 When you look in a mirror, you see a **reflection** of yourself.

2 A **reflection** of something is also a copy where everything is the other way round.

a b c d e f g h i j k l m n o p q **Rr** s t u v w x y z

a
b
c
d
e
f
g
h
i
j
k
l
m
n
o
p
q
Rr
s
t
u
v
w
x
y
z

refrigerator **refrigerators**
You keep food cold and fresh in a large metal cupboard called a **refrigerator**. A **refrigerator** is often called a fridge.

refuse **refuses, refusing, refused**
If you **refuse** to do something, you say that you will not do it.
Mum asked if I would like to go shopping, but I refused.

remember **remembers, remembering, remembered**
If you **remember** something, you can bring it back to your mind.
I can remember my first day at school.

remind **reminds, reminding, reminded**
If you **remind** someone to do something, you make them remember to do it.
Liam reminded me to take my book home.

remove **removes, removing, removed**
If you **remove** something, you take it away.
Please remove your bags from the floor.

repair **repairs, repairing, repaired**
If you **repair** something that is broken, you mend it.

repeat **repeats, repeating, repeated**
When something is **repeated**, it happens all over again.
I'm going to watch that programme again when it is repeated next week.

reply **replies, replying, replied**
1 If you **reply** to something, you give an answer.
I haven't replied to Annie's invitation yet.
2 A **reply** is the answer you give.
I haven't sent a reply yet.

*Dear Annie
I can/can not come to your party from Ian*

report **reports**
A **report** tells you the facts about something.
We read a book on goldfish and then wrote a report on how to look after them.

represent **represents, representing, represented**
A letter or symbol that takes the place of a number or word **represents** it.

reptile **reptiles**
A **reptile** is an animal with cold blood and scaly skin. **Reptiles** have short legs or no legs at all. They usually lay eggs.

rescue **rescues, rescuing, rescued**
If you **rescue** someone, you save them from danger.
The farmer rescued the cow from the river.

rest rests, resting, rested

1 When you **rest**, you are quiet and do nothing for a while.
Gran is resting in her chair.

2 You have a **rest** when you sit or lie down quietly.
Gran always has a rest after lunch.

3 The **rest** of something is all that remains of it.
I ate half the cake and couldn't finish the rest.

restaurant restaurants

You can buy and eat a meal at a **restaurant**.

result results

A **result** is what happens because something else has happened.
Alex missed his bus, and as a result was late for school.

retell retells, retelling, retold

If you **retell** a story, you tell it again in a new way.
This story has been retold all over the world.

return returns, returning, returned

1 If you **return**, you go back to the place where you were before.
Mum has just returned home from work.

2 If you **return** something to someone, you give it back to them.
I'll return Jim's book when I've read it.

reward rewards, rewarding, rewarded

You can be given a **reward** for doing something well.
The police gave Jason a reward for finding the gold watch.

rhinoceros rhinoceroses

A **rhinoceros**, or **rhino**, is a large wild animal. It has one or two horns on its nose. **Rhinoceroses** live in Africa and Asia.

rhyme rhymes, rhyming, rhymed

1 Words that **rhyme** end with the same sound, like *bean* and *green*.

2 A **rhyme** is a short rhyming poem.

rhythm rhythms

A **rhythm** is a repeated pattern of sound in music or poetry.

ribbon ribbons

A **ribbon** is a long, narrow piece of coloured material.
I put yellow ribbon around the parcel.

rice

Rice is a plant that grows in hot countries. You can cook and eat the seeds of the **rice** plant.

rich richer, richest

A **rich** person has a lot of money.

riddle riddles

A **riddle** is a difficult question with a funny answer.
Here is a riddle. What gets bigger the more you take away? A hole!

a
b
c
d
e
f
g
h
i
j
k
l
m
n
o
p
q
Rr
s
t
u
v
w
x
y
z

a
b
c
d
e
f
g
h
i
j
k
l
m
n
o
p
q
Rr
s
t
u
v
w
x
y
z

ride   rides, riding, rode, ridden
1 If you **ride** a bike or a horse, you sit on it and control how it moves.
2 When you **ride** in a bus, car or train, you travel in it.

right
1 **Right** means the opposite of left.
*Tom has his **right** foot on the ball.*
2 **Right** also means correct.
*Well done! You got all your sums **right**.*
3 **Right** can also mean exactly.
*Stand **right** in the middle of the circle.*

right angle   right angles
A **right angle** is an angle of 90 degrees. The symbol for it is a small square.
*The sides of a square meet at **right angles**.*

ring   rings, ringing, rang, rung
1 A **ring** is a small circle of metal that you wear on your finger.
2 When you shake or press a bell and it makes a noise, it **rings**.

ripe   riper, ripest
When fruit is **ripe**, it is ready to eat.
*That tomato is still green because it isn't **ripe** yet.*

rise   rises, rising, rose, risen
1 If something **rises**, it moves upwards.
2 If you **rise**, you stand up.

river   rivers
A **river** is water that flows through the land to a sea or a lake.

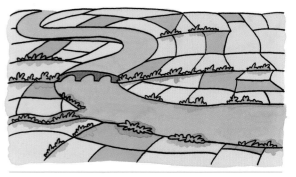

road   roads
A **road** is a long piece of hard ground. Cars and other vehicles travel along **roads**.

roar   roars
A **roar** is a deep, loud noise like a lion makes.

robin   robins
A **robin** is a small brown bird with a red breast.

robot   robots
A **robot** is a machine controlled by a computer. **Robots** can move and do jobs that people usually do.
*A lot of cars are made by **robots**.*

rock   rocks, rocking, rocked
1 **Rock** is the very hard material that the surface of the Earth is made of. Pieces of this are called **rocks**.
2 If you **rock** something, you move it gently from side to side.

rocket   rockets
1 A **rocket** is a vehicle shaped like a pointed tube that goes into space.
2 A **rocket** is also a firework that explodes high up in the sky.

rod rods

A **rod** is a long, thin piece of wood or metal. **Rods** are used for fishing.

rode See **ride**.

roll rolls, rolling, rolled

1 When an object such as a wheel moves across a surface, it **rolls**.
2 A **roll** of something is a long piece wrapped round and round on itself. Sticky tape comes on a **roll**.
3 A bread **roll** is a small, round piece of bread.

roof roofs

The **roof** of a building or car is the top part of it.

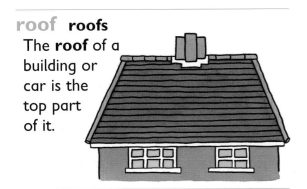

room rooms

A **room** is part of a building. It has its own walls, floor and ceiling.

root roots

A **root** is the part of a plant that grows under the ground.

rope ropes

Rope is a very thick, strong type of string. It is made by twisting together many threads.

rose roses

A **rose** is a beautiful garden flower with a lovely smell.

rough rougher, roughest

1 If something is **rough**, it is bumpy and not smooth.
2 **Rough** weather is stormy and not quiet.

roughly

Roughly means about but not exactly.
*I'll be there at **roughly** five o'clock.*

round

Something **round** has a shape like a circle or a ball.

roundabout roundabouts

1 Where roads cross, you often find a **roundabout**. Vehicles go around the **roundabout** until they reach the road they want.
2 A **roundabout** is a ride at a fair.

route routes

Your **route** is how you get from one place to another.
*There are two **routes** from here to my house.*

row rows, rowing, rowed

1 (*sounds like* toe) A **row** is a line of things or people side by side.
2 (*sounds like* toe) When you **row** a boat, you move it through the water using oars.

3 (*sounds like* cow) When people are angry and shout at each other, they are having a **row**.

a b c d e f g h i j k l m n o p q **Rr** s t u v w x y z

a
b
c
d
e
f
g
h
i
j
k
l
m
n
o
p
q
Rr
s
t
u
v
w
x
y
z

royal
Queens, kings and members of their family are **royal**. They are all members of the **royal** family.

rub **rubs, rubbing, rubbed**
1 If you **rub** something, you move your hand, or something you are holding, backwards and forwards across it.
I rubbed my shoes until they shone.
2 If you **rub** something out, you make it disappear by **rubbing** it.
I rubbed out my writing and started again.

rubber **rubbers**
1 **Rubber** is a strong, stretchy material. Car tyres and wellington boots are made of **rubber**.
2 You use a **rubber** to get rid of pencil marks on paper.

rubbish
Rubbish is the things that you throw away.

ruby **rubies**
A **ruby** is a red jewel.

rude **ruder, rudest**
A **rude** person behaves badly and is not polite.
It is rude to call people names!

rug **rugs**
1 A **rug** is a small, thick carpet.
2 A **rug** is also a blanket which you can sit on outdoors or wrap around you to keep warm.

ruin **ruins, ruining, ruined**
1 If you **ruin** something, you spoil it completely.
The rain ruined our holiday.
2 A **ruin** is a building that is almost completely destroyed.

rule **rules, ruling, ruled**
1 A **rule** describes what you must do or what always happens.
Eating in the library is against the rules.
2 Someone who **rules** a country tells everybody else what to do.

ruler **rulers**
1 A **ruler** is used for measuring or for drawing straight lines.

cm | 1 | 2 | 3 | 4 | 5 | 6 | 7 | 8 | 9 | 10

2 A **ruler** is also someone who rules a country.

run **runs, running, ran, run**
1 When you **run**, you move quickly and both your feet come off the ground at once.
2 If you **run** a bath, you turn on the taps and fill it up.
3 A **run** is a point in cricket or baseball.

rung See **ring**.

rush **rushes, rushing, rushed**
1 If you **rush**, you do something or go somewhere very quickly.
We rushed to the shops before they closed.
2 If you are in a **rush**, you are busy and do not have enough time to do things.

sack sacks
A **sack** is a large bag. It is made of cloth or plastic and used to carry or store things in.
*The **sack** of potatoes was heavy.*

sad sadder, saddest
If you are **sad**, you do not feel happy.
*I was very **sad** when we left our old house.*

saddle saddles
You sit on a **saddle** when you ride a horse or a bicycle.

safe safer, safest; safes
1 If someone or something is **safe**, they are not in danger.
*Lock your bike in the garage. It will be **safe** there.*
2 A **safe** is a strong metal box with special locks. You can keep money and valuable things in a **safe**.

said See **say**.

sail sails, sailing, sailed
1 A **sail** is a large piece of cloth fixed onto a boat. The boat is moved through the water by the wind blowing into the **sails**.
2 If you **sail**, you travel in a boat.
*We are **sailing** on the four o'clock ferry.*

sailor sailors
A **sailor** works on a ship.

salad salads
Salad is a mixture of raw vegetables and other things, eaten cold.

sale sales
During a **sale**, shops sell things at lower prices.
*Mum bought my coat for half price in the **sale**.*

salt
Salt is a white powder that is used to flavour food. **Salt** is found in the ground and in sea water.

same
1 If two things are the **same**, they are exactly like each other.
2 If things happen at the **same** time, they happen together exactly.

sand
Sand is a powder made from very tiny bits of rock. **Sand** is found on beaches and in deserts.

sandal sandals
A **sandal** is a light, open shoe that you wear in warm weather.

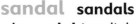

a b c d e f g h i j k l m n o p q r **Ss** t u v w x y z

127

a
b
c
d
e
f
g
h
i
j
k
l
m
n
o
p
q
r
Ss
t
u
v
w
x
y
z

sandpit sandpits
A **sandpit** is a box filled with sand for children to dig in.

sandwich sandwiches
You make a **sandwich** by putting a filling between two pieces of bread.

sang See **sing**.

sank See **sink**.

sari saris
A **sari** is a piece of of clothing worn by Indian women. It is a long piece of material folded around the body in a special way.

sat See **sit**.

satellite satellites
A **satellite** is something that is sent into space to travel round and round the Earth. **Satellites** send back new information or pass signals from one part of the Earth to another.
The television pictures came from Australia by satellite.

Saturday Saturdays
Saturday is the day of the week between Friday and Sunday.

sauce sauces
A **sauce** is a thick, cooked liquid. It is served with food to give it more flavour.
My favourite meal is fish fingers, chips and peas covered in tomato sauce.

saucepan saucepans
A **saucepan** is a deep metal pot with a long handle and a lid. You cook food in a **saucepan**.

saucer saucers
A **saucer** is a small, round plate that you put a cup on.

sausage sausages
A **sausage** is made from very tiny pieces of meat put into a skin.

save saves, saving, saved
1 If you **save** someone, you stop them from being hurt or killed.
My mum saved me from drowning.
2 If you **save** your money, you keep it so that you can spend it later.

saw saws
1 A **saw** is a tool for cutting wood. It has a blade with sharp teeth.
2 *I saw a puppy at the park.* See **see**.

say says, saying, said
When you **say** something, you make words with your voice.

scale scales
1 You weigh something using a set of **scales.**
2 A fish is covered in **scales**. A **scale** is a piece of hard skin.

scare scares, scaring, scared
If something **scares** you, you feel frightened.

scared
When you are **scared,** you are afraid.
Our dog is scared of fireworks.

scarf scarfs or scarves
A **scarf** is a long piece of material. You wear it around your neck to keep you warm.

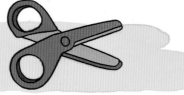

scent scents
The **scent** of something is what it smells like.

school schools
Children go to **school** to learn.

science sciences
When you learn about **science**, you find out about plants and animals. You also learn about materials like water and metal, and things like sound, light and electricity.

scissors
You use **scissors** to cut paper or cloth. They have two sharp blades and handles with holes for your fingers.

score scores, scoring, scored
1 You **score** a goal at football by putting the ball into the net.
2 The number of points the teams have in a match is called the **score**.

scratch scratches, scratching, scratched
1 If you **scratch** something, you make marks with something sharp.
The cat scratched the table with her claws.
2 A **scratch** is a mark or small cut.

scream screams, screaming, screamed
If you **scream**, you give a loud high shout because you are frightened or excited.

screech screeches, screeching, screeched
When something **screeches**, it makes a loud, high noise.
The brakes screeched as the car came to a sudden stop.

screen screens
A **screen** is the part of a television or computer where the pictures or writing appear.

screw screws, screwing, screwed
1 A **screw** is a thin, pointed piece of metal. It looks like a nail but you put it in by turning it round and round.
2 If you **screw** things together, you fix them together using **screws**.

sea seas
The **sea** is the salty water that covers most of the Earth's surface.

a b c d e f g h i j k l m n o p q r **Ss** t u v w x y z

seal seals
A **seal** is an animal with short fur. **Seals** live in the sea and on land.

search searches, searching, searched
If you **search** for something, you look carefully for it.
I've searched everywhere for my watch but I can't find it!

seaside
The **seaside** is any place beside the sea.

season seasons
The year is divided into four parts called **seasons**. The four **seasons** are called spring, summer, autumn and winter.

seat seats
A **seat** is somewhere that you sit.

Ss

second seconds
1 A **second** is a small amount of time. There are 60 **seconds** in a minute.
2 The **second** in a list of things comes just after the first.

secret secrets
A **secret** is something that only a few people know about.
Mum's birthday party is a secret.

see sees, seeing, saw, seen
1 When you **see** something, your eyes notice it.
2 If you go to **see** someone, you visit them.

seed seeds
A **seed** is a small, hard object in the fruit of a plant. When it is ripe, it can grow in the ground into a new plant.

seek seeks, seeking, sought
If you **seek** something, you look for it.
The pirate was seeking the buried treasure.

seem seems, seeming, seemed
If something **seems** to be true, it looks as if it is true.
Bronwen seems shy, but she's not.
The cat seems to be hungry.

seen See **see**.

seesaw seesaws
A **seesaw** is an outdoor toy. One child sits at each end of a long piece of wood. They go up and down in turn.

selfish
Selfish people only care about themselves.

sell   sells, selling, sold
When you **sell** something, you give it to someone who pays you money for it.

semicircle   semicircles
A **semicircle** is exactly half a circle.

send   sends, sending, sent
When you **send** something to a place, you make it go there.
Mum sent me upstairs to wash my hands.

sense   senses
People have five **senses**. They can hear, see, taste, feel and smell.

sensible
Sensible people are good at knowing what is the best thing to do.

sent   See **send**.

sentence   sentences
A **sentence** is a group of words that tell you something. When you write a **sentence** down, you begin with a capital letter and end with a full stop.

separate   separates, separating, separated
1 Two things that are **separate** are not connected in any way.
2 You **separate** things when you make them come apart.

September
September is the ninth month of the year. It has 30 days.

sequence   sequences
A **sequence** is a group of things that come in a certain order.
*What is the next number in the **sequence** 5, 10, 15?*

serve   serves, serving, served
1 If you **serve** food or drink to someone, you give it to them.
2 Someone who **serves** in a shop helps people to buy what they want.

set   sets, setting, set
1 A **set** is a group of things that belong together.
*Shall we get out the chess **set**?*
2 When something **sets**, it goes hard or firm.
*We'll turn out the jelly when it's **set**.*

several
Several means more than two but not many.

sew   sews, sewing, sewed, sewn
If you **sew**, you use a needle and thread to join two things together.
Mum is sewing a button onto my coat.

sex   sexes
People and animals are divided into two groups, males and females. These groups are called the **sexes**.

a
b
c
d
e
f
g
h
i
j
k
l
m
n
o
p
q
r
Ss
t
u
v
w
x
y
z

a b c d e f g h i j k l m n o p q r **Ss** t u v w x y z

shade

If you are in the **shade**, you are in a place that the sunlight does not reach.

It's too hot. Let's sit in the shade of that umbrella.

shadow   shadows

If you stand in front of the light, you make a dark shape called a **shadow**.

shake   shakes, shaking, shook, shaken

If you **shake** something, you move it quickly from side to side.

shallow   shallower, shallowest

Something **shallow** is not very deep.

Amy sat in a shallow pool.

shampoo   shampoos

Shampoo is the soapy liquid you use for washing your hair.

shape   shapes

The **shape** of something is the pattern made by its outside edges. You use words like *square, oval* and *cone* to describe the **shapes** of things.

You can see lots of shapes on page 184.

share   shares, sharing, shared

1 When something is divided between two or more people, it is **shared**.

2 Each person gets a **share** of something that is divided up between them.

shark   sharks

A **shark** is a large, powerful fish with a lot of sharp teeth. **Sharks** live in the sea.

sharp   sharper, sharpest

1 Something **sharp** can cut or prick things easily.

A knife has a sharp edge.

A pin has a sharp point.

2 A **sharp** change is very sudden.

There was a sharp bend in the road.

shave   shaves, shaving, shaved

When someone **shaves**, they cut the hair from their skin to make it smooth.

shed   sheds, shedding, shed

1 A **shed** is a small building. People store garden tools in a **shed**.

2 If you **shed** something, you take it off or let it fall off.

Trees shed their leaves in the autumn.

sheep   sheep

A **sheep** is a farm animal that eats grass. **Sheep** are kept for wool and meat.

sheet sheets
1 A **sheet** is a large piece of thin cloth that you put on a bed.
2 A **sheet** of paper or glass is a piece of it.

shelf shelves
A **shelf** is a long, flat piece of wood fixed to a wall. You keep things like books on **shelves**.

shell shells
A **shell** is the hard outer part of a nut, egg or seed. Animals like snails, crabs and tortoises have **shells**, too.
*The **shells** you pick up on the beach used to be the **shells** of little creatures.*

shelter shelters, sheltering, sheltered
1 A **shelter** is a place that protects you.
*I stood in the bus **shelter** to keep dry.*
2 If you **shelter** from the rain, you stay somewhere dry.

shelves See **shelf**.

shepherd shepherds
A **shepherd** looks after sheep.

shin shins
Your **shin** is the front of your leg below the knee. (See page 174.)

shine shines, shining, shone or shined
1 When something **shines,** it gives out bright light.
2 When you **shine** an object, you rub it to make it bright.

shiny shinier, shiniest
Shiny things are bright.

ship ships
A **ship** is a large boat. **Ships** carry people and things across the sea.

shirt shirts
A **shirt** is a piece of clothing that you wear on the top part of your body. It often has a collar and buttons.

shiver shivers, shivering, shivered
When you **shiver**, your body shakes, usually because you are cold.

shoe shoes
You wear **shoes** on your feet. They are usually made of leather or plastic and have a hard bottom surface.

shoelace shoelaces
A **shoelace** is used to fasten some shoes. It goes through holes in the front of the shoe and is tied in a bow.

Ss

a b c d e f g h i j k l m n o p q r s t u v w x y z

a
b
c
d
e
f
g
h
i
j
k
l
m
n
o
p
q
r
Ss
t
u
v
w
x
y
z

shone See **shine**.

shook See **shake**.

shoot shoots, shooting, shot
1 If someone **shoots**, they make something go very fast out of a gun or a bow.
2 A **shoot** is the part of a plant that you see when it first comes up through the ground.

shop shops, shopping, shopped
1 A **shop** is a place where things are sold.
2 When you **shop**, you go to the **shops** to buy things.

shore shores
The **shore** is the flat land at the edge of a sea or lake.

short shorter, shortest
1 A **short** person is not very tall.
2 Something **short** is not very long.
*My story is very **short**, so it will only take a few minutes to read.*

shorts
Shorts are short trousers that end above the knees. (See page 177.)

shot See **shoot**.

shoulder shoulders
Your **shoulder** is where your arm joins your body. (See page 174.)

shout shouts, shouting, shouted
1 If you **shout**, you call out loudly.
2 A **shout** is a loud call or cry.

show shows, showing, showed, shown
1 If you **show** something to someone, you let them see it.
2 If you **show** someone how to do something, you let them watch you doing it.
3 If you see a **show**, you watch something for fun.

shower showers
1 If you have a **shower**, you stand under a spray of water in the bathroom and wash yourself.
2 A **shower** is rain or snow that only falls for a short time.

shown See **show**.

shrink shrinks, shrinking, shrank, shrunk
If something **shrinks**, it becomes smaller.

shut **shuts, shutting, shut**
If you **shut** something, you move part of it so that it is no longer open.
Shut the door to keep out the cold.

shy **shyer, shyest**
A **shy** person is nervous about meeting people.
My baby sister is so shy that she cries if someone new talks to her!

sick
Someone who is **sick** is ill.
Our teacher has been away for a week because he is sick.

side **sides**
1 A **side** is the left or right part of something.

2 The **sides** of an object can also be its flat faces.

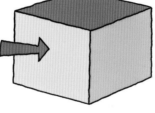

3 A **side** of a flat shape is the straight line between two corners.

4 A team of players in a match can be called a **side**.

sideways
If you move **sideways**, you go to your left or right but keep facing forwards.

sigh **sighs, sighing, sighed**
When you **sigh**, you breathe out slowly and make a sad sound. People **sigh** when they are sad, bored or tired.

sign **signs**
A **sign** is a notice that gives you information using words or pictures.

signal **signals**
1 A **signal** is a sound or action that tells people something.
When I blow my whistle, that's the signal for the end of playtime.
2 A railway **signal** tells train drivers whether they can go or must stop.

silent
If you are **silent**, you make no noise.

silk
Silk is a smooth, shiny cloth. It is made from threads spun by a silkworm.

silly **sillier, silliest**
A **silly** person is not being sensible.
It was silly of you to go out in the rain without a coat!

silver
Silver is a shiny, grey metal. It is often used to make rings and earrings.

sing **sings, singing, sang, sung**
When you **sing**, you make musical sounds with your voice.
Harry is singing his favourite song.

a b c d e f g h i j k l m n o p q r **Ss** t u v w x y z

135

a
b
c
d
e
f
g
h
i
j
k
l
m
n
o
p
q
r
Ss
t
u
v
w
x
y
z

single

Single means only one and not more.

*We won the match by a **single** point.*

singular

You use the **singular** form of a word when you are talking about one person or thing.

*The **singular** of "children" is "child".*

sink   sinks, sinking, sank, sunk

1 If something **sinks**, it moves downwards through water.

2 You can wash up in the kitchen **sink**.

sip   sips, sipping, sipped

If you **sip** a drink, you take it a little at a time.

sister   sisters

Your **sister** is a girl who has the same parents as you.

sit   sits, sitting, sat

When you **sit**, you rest your bottom on something.

size   sizes

The **size** of something is how big it is.

*The popcorn comes in three **sizes** – small, medium and large. Which **size** do you want?*

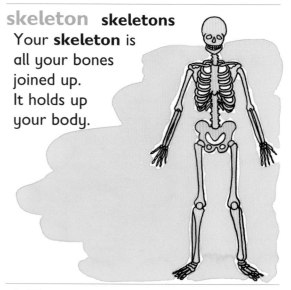

Small   Medium   Large

skate   skates

A **skate** is a special boot. An ice **skate** has a blade fixed under it and a roller **skate** has wheels.

*The blade on one of my ice **skates** is broken.*

skateboard   skateboards

A **skateboard** is a board on wheels. You stand on it with both feet.

skeleton   skeletons

Your **skeleton** is all your bones joined up. It holds up your body.

skill   skills

If you have a **skill**, you can do something well.

*Reading and writing are very useful **skills**.*

skin

Your **skin** covers the outside of your body. Animals have many different kinds of **skin**. Some fruit and vegetables have **skin**, too.

*I peeled the banana and threw away the **skin**.*

skip   skips, skipping, skipped

When you **skip**, you move forwards with little jumps from one foot to the other. Sometimes you **skip** with a rope.

skirt **skirts**
A **skirt** is a piece of clothing worn by girls and women. It hangs down from the waist. (See page 176.)

skull **skulls**
Your **skull** is the bony part of your head. Your brain is inside your **skull**.

sky **skies**
The **sky** is the space above the Earth where you see the sun, clouds and stars.

sledge **sledges**
You use a **sledge** to slide over snow. A large **sledge** is sometimes pulled by dogs.

sleep **sleeps, sleeping, slept**
When you **sleep**, your eyes are closed and you do not know what is happening around you.

sleeve **sleeves**
A **sleeve** is the part of a jacket, shirt or blouse that covers your arm.

slept See **sleep**.

slice **slices**
A **slice** is a thin piece cut from something bigger.
*May I have another **slice** of bread, please?*

slide **slides, sliding, slid**
1 When something **slides**, it moves quickly over a smooth surface.
2 A **slide** is an outdoor toy. You climb to the top and **slide** down.

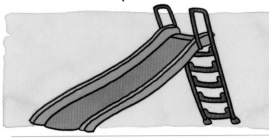

slip **slips, slipping, slipped**
If you **slip**, you fall down because you slide by accident.

slipper **slippers**
Slippers are soft shoes that you wear indoors.

slippery
If something is **slippery**, it is difficult to hold or walk on because it is wet or very smooth.
On an icy day, the playground is very slippery.

slope **slopes**
A **slope** is a piece of ground or a surface that is higher at one end than the other.

slow **slower, slowest**
If something is **slow**, it takes a long time.

slowly
If you do something **slowly**, you take a long time to do it.

a b c d e f g h i j k l m n o p q r **Ss** t u v w x y z

137

slug slugs

A **slug** is a small animal that moves slowly. It is like a snail without its shell.

small smaller, smallest

A **small** person or thing is not very big.

A mouse is a small animal.

smart smarter, smartest

1 If you look **smart**, you look neat and tidy.

2 **Smart** also means clever.

smash smashes, smashing, smashed

If something **smashes**, it breaks into lots of pieces.

Dad dropped the cup and it smashed on the floor.

smell smells, smelling, smelled or smelt

1 When you **smell** something, you notice it with your nose.

I could smell something burning.

2 You notice a **smell** by using your nose.

There was a smell of burning.

smile smiles, smiling, smiled

1 When you **smile**, your face looks happy.

2 A **smile** is a look of happiness on your face.

smoke

Smoke is the white or grey cloud that goes into the air when something burns.

When Dad lit the bonfire, smoke filled the air.

smooth smoother, smoothest

If something is **smooth**, it has no lumps or rough bits.

Toads have bumps, but frogs are smooth.

snack snacks

A **snack** is a small, quick meal.

We had a couple of sandwiches as a snack.

snail snails

A **snail** is a small, soft creature with a shell on its back. It moves very slowly.

snake snakes

A **snake** is a long, thin reptile with scales and no legs. Some **snakes** are dangerous to humans.

snap snaps, snapping, snapped

If something **snaps**, it breaks suddenly with a sharp noise.

A twig snapped under my foot.

sneeze **sneezes, sneezing, sneezed**
When you **sneeze**, you suddenly push air out through your nose, making a loud noise.
I had a bad cold and couldn't stop sneezing.

snow **snows, snowing, snowed**
1 Snow is soft, white frozen water that falls from the sky when it is cold.
2 It **snows** when **snow** falls from the sky.

snowball **snowballs**
A **snowball** is a small ball of snow. People make **snowballs** and throw them at each other for fun.

snowflake **snowflakes**
A **snowflake** is a single piece of snow as it falls.

snowman **snowmen**
A **snowman** is snow made into the shape of a person.

soak **soaks, soaking, soaked**
If you **soak** something, you leave it in liquid.
Mum soaked my dirty socks in water overnight.

soap **soaps**
You use **soap** and water to wash yourself or your clothes.

sock **socks**
You wear **socks** on your feet to keep them warm. (See page 177.)

sofa **sofas**
A **sofa** is a long, soft seat with arms and a back. Two or three people can sit on a **sofa**.

soft **softer, softest**
If something is **soft**, it sinks down when you press it.
My head sank into the soft pillow.

soil
Soil is the top layer of earth that plants grow in.

sold See **sell**.

soldier **soldiers**
A **soldier** belongs to an army.

solid
1 A **solid** material feels firm and does not change shape easily.
Wood is solid but oil and water are liquid.
2 Something **solid** is not hollow.

solve **solves, solving, solved**
If you **solve** a problem, you find the answer to it.

a b c d e f g h i j k l m n o p q r **Ss** t u v w x y z

some

a
b
c
d
e
f
g
h
i
j
k
l
m
n
o
p
q
r
Ss
t
u
v
w
x
y
z

some

You say **some** when you mean a number or amount but do not say it exactly.

*Please pass me **some** sausages and **some** mashed potato.*

somebody

Somebody is a person you do not name.

***Somebody** has left their coat behind.*

someone

Someone is another word for somebody.

something

Something is a thing that you do not describe.

*I can hear **something** banging.*

sometimes

Sometimes means quite often but not always.

*I'm **sometimes** allowed to stay up late on holiday.*

somewhere

If you say you went **somewhere**, you do not say exactly where.

son sons

A person's **son** is their male child.

*Mr Jones has two **sons**.*

song songs

When you sing a **song**, you sing words to a piece of music.

soon sooner, soonest

Soon means not too long into the future.

*Today is Friday. **Soon** it will be the weekend.*

sore

If part of your body is **sore**, it hurts.

*I have a **sore** throat – it hurts when I swallow.*

sorry

You say that you are **sorry** when you have done something wrong.

*I'm **sorry** I'm late.*

sort sorts, sorting, sorted

1 If things are the same **sort**, they are the same kind.

*Do you like this **sort** of chocolate?*

2 If you **sort** things, you put them into groups.

***Sort** these buttons into two piles – red ones and blue ones.*

sought See **seek**.

sound sounds

A **sound** is something you can hear.

*Can you hear the **sound** of the drums?*

soup soups

Soup is a hot liquid food made from meat or vegetables.

sour

If something is **sour**, it has a sharp taste like a lemon.

*This milk tastes **sour**. Throw it away.*

south

South is a direction. It is on your right when you look towards the rising sun.

space   spaces

1 A **space** is a gap or an empty place.

*Is there a **space** for me at your table?*

2 Space is all around the Earth where the planets and the stars are.

spaceship   spaceships

A **spaceship** is a vehicle that can travel through space.

spade   spades

A **spade** is a tool used for digging. It has a long handle and a wide blade.

sparrow   sparrows

A **sparrow** is a small brown bird found in many parts of the world.

speak   speaks, speaking, spoke, spoken

When you **speak**, you say words out loud.

special

If something is **special**, it is better than other things of the same kind.

*Mum made a **special** meal for my birthday.*

speech

Speech is what you hear when someone is speaking.

speech marks

Speech marks are marks you use in writing to show when someone starts and stops speaking.

"I'm going out now," said Dad.

"Can I come?" I asked.

speech marks

speed   speeds

The **speed** of something is how fast it is moving.

*The racing car was travelling at a very high **speed**.*

spell   spells, spelling, spelled or spelt

1 When you **spell** a word, you say or write the letters in the right order.

*Please **spell** your name.*

2 In fairy stories, if someone says a **spell**, magic things happen.

a
b
c
d
e
f
g
h
i
j
k
l
m
n
o
p
q
r
Ss
t
u
v
w
x
y
z

a
b
c
d
e
f
g
h
i
j
k
l
m
n
o
p
q
r

Ss

t
u
v
w
x
y
z

spend   spends, spending, spent
1 You **spend** money when you buy something with it.
2 You **spend** time when you use it.
I spent three hours painting.

sphere   spheres
A **sphere** is an object that is round when you look at it from any direction. Footballs and planets are **spheres**.

spider   spiders
A **spider** is a small animal with eight legs. It spins a web to catch insects for food.

spill   spills, spilling, spilled or spilt
If you **spill** something, it runs out of a container by mistake.
I spilt my drink all over my shirt!

spin   spins, spinning, spun
If something **spins**, it turns round very quickly.
The washing machine spins our clothes.

spine   spines
1 Your **spine** is the long row of bones down the middle of your back.
2 A **spine** is a long, sharp point on an animal's body or a plant.

spiteful
A **spiteful** person says nasty things to people.

splash   splashes
When something hits the water, it makes a **splash**.

split   splits, splitting, split
If something **splits**, it divides into parts.

spoil   spoils, spoiling, spoiled, spoilt
If something is **spoilt**, it is not as good as it was before.

spoke   See **speak**.

spoon   spoons
You use a **spoon** to eat soup and cereal, and to stir liquids.

sport   sports
A **sport** is something that you do to keep fit and to have fun. Swimming, rounders and football are all **sports**.

spot   spots
1 A **spot** is a round mark.
A ladybird is red with black spots.
2 A **spot** is also a small red mark on your skin.

spout   spouts
You pour the water out of a jug or kettle through its **spout**.

spray **sprays, spraying, sprayed**
If you **spray** something, you make it wet with tiny drops of liquid.

spring **springs**
1 Spring is the season between winter and summer. The weather gets warmer and plants start to grow again.
2 A **spring** is a curly piece of metal. It jumps back to its normal shape after you press it down.

spun See **spin**.

square **squares**
1 A **square** is a shape with four equal sides and four corners that are all right angles.
2 Anything that has this shape is **square**.

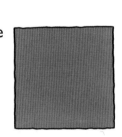

squash **squashes, squashing, squashed**
1 Squash is a drink made from fruit, sugar and water.
2 If you **squash** something, you press it so that it goes flat.
*Emily sat on her hat and **squashed** it flat.*

squeak **squeaks, squeaking, squeaked**
If something **squeaks**, it makes a short, high noise.
*My new shoes **squeak** when I walk.*

squeeze **squeezes, squeezing, squeezed**
If you **squeeze** something, you press its sides together.
*Mum **squeezed** the oranges to get the juice out.*

squirrel **squirrels**
A **squirrel** is a small animal with a long, thick tail. **Squirrels** live in trees and eat nuts.

stable **stables**
A horse is kept in a **stable**.

stage **stages**
A **stage** is a raised platform in a theatre or hall.
*At the pantomime, there was a horse on the **stage**.*

stair **stairs**
Stairs are a set of steps inside a building. You climb the **stairs** from one floor to the next.

stamp **stamps**
A **stamp** is a small piece of paper with a picture on it. You stick a **stamp** on a letter or parcel before you post it.

stand **stands, standing, stood**
When you **stand**, your feet stay in one place on the floor.

a b c d e f g h i j k l m n o p q r **Ss** t u v w x y z

143

a b c d e f g h i j k l m n o p q r **Ss** t u v w x y z

star stars
1 A **star** is a tiny light in the sky at night.
2 A **star** is also a famous actor or performer.
3 A **star** can also be a shape with five or more points. (See page 184.)

stare stares, staring, stared
1 If you **stare** at something, you look at it for a long time.
2 A **stare** is a long look at something.

start starts, starting, started
If you **start** to do something, you begin to do it.
I've just started my homework.

station stations
1 Trains and buses stop for passengers at a **station**.
2 A **station** is also a building with a special use, like a police **station**.
We went to the petrol station for some petrol.

statue statues
A **statue** is a figure of a person or animal. **Statues** are made from stone or metal.

stay stays, staying, stayed
1 If you **stay** in a place, you do not move away from it.
2 If you **stay** in a hotel, you sleep there.

steady steadier, steadiest
If something is **steady**, it does not shake or move.
Please hold the ladder steady.

steal steals, stealing, stole, stolen
If you **steal** something, you take something that belongs to someone else.

steam
Steam is the white cloud you see above very hot water. It is made of tiny drops of water.
Steam was coming off the hot tea.

steel
Steel is a strong metal.

steep steeper, steepest
A **steep** slope goes up sharply.
We pushed our bikes up the hill because it was too steep to ride them.

stem stems
The **stem** of a plant holds the leaves and flowers away from the soil.

step steps, stepping, stepped
1 You **step** when you move your foot up and down when you walk.
2 A **step** is also where you put your foot on the stairs or a ladder.
There are 12 steps up to Gran's flat.

stereo **stereos**
A **stereo** is a machine for playing tapes and CDs.

stick **sticks, sticking, stuck**
1 A **stick** is a long, thin piece of wood.
2 If you **stick** one thing to another, you fix it with glue or tape.
3 If you **stick** a pointed object into something, you push it in so that it stays there.

stiff **stiffer, stiffest**
If something is **stiff**, it is hard to bend.
*The boxes were made of **stiff** cardboard.*

still
1 If something is **still** happening, it has not stopped yet.
*It's been raining all day and it's **still** raining.*
2 If you are **still**, you are not moving.
*Stand **still** while I button your coat.*

sting **stings, stinging, stung**
If something **stings** you, it pricks your skin and hurts you.
*A bee **stung** Anya in the arm.*

stir **stirs, stirring, stirred**
When you **stir** a liquid, you use a spoon or a stick to move it around.

stole See **steal**.

stolen See **steal**.

stomach **stomachs**
When you swallow your food, it goes into your **stomach**.

stone **stones**
1 **Stone** is a hard, dry material. It is used for building houses and walls. You find small **stones** on the ground.
2 The hard seed in the middle of a peach or a plum is called a **stone**.

stood See **stand**.

stop **stops, stopping, stopped**
1 If you **stop** doing something, you do not do it any more.
2 If someone **stops** you doing something, they do not let you do it.
3 A bus lets people on or off at a bus **stop**.

store **stores, storing, stored**
1 If you **store** something, you keep it until it is needed.
2 A **store** is a large shop which sells lots of different things.

storm **storms**
In a **storm** it rains hard and strong winds blow. There is often thunder and lightning.

a b c d e f g h i j k l m n o p q r **Ss** t u v w x y z

a
b
c
d
e
f
g
h
i
j
k
l
m
n
o
p
q
r

Ss

t
u
v
w
x
y
z

story   stories
A **story** tells you about people and what happened to them. Some **stories** are made up, others are about real people.

straight   straighter, straightest
Something **straight** is not bent or curved.
*Lisa has **straight** hair.*

strange   stranger, strangest
Something **strange** seems odd and unusual.
*The alien had **strange** yellow eyes.*

straw   straws
1 Farm animals sleep on **straw**. It is the dry stems from wheat and corn.
2 A **straw** is a thin plastic tube that you can drink through.

strawberry   strawberries
A **strawberry** is a small, soft, red fruit. It has tiny seeds on its surface.

stream   streams
A **stream** is a small river.

street   streets
A **street** is a road in a town. It has shops and houses along it.

strength
Your **strength** is your energy and power.
*I haven't got the **strength** to lift that suitcase.*

stretch   stretches, stretching, stretched
When you **stretch** something, you pull it to make it longer or wider.
*David **stretched** the rubber band.*

strict   stricter, strictest
A **strict** person makes people behave well and do what they should.

string   strings
1 String is thin rope used for tying things together.
2 You play on the **strings** of violins and guitars to make music.

strip   strips
A **strip** is a long, thin piece of something.

stripe   stripes
A **stripe** is a line on something.
*Zebras have **stripes** on their bodies.*

strong   stronger, strongest
1 A **strong** person can lift heavy things.
2 You cannot easily break something that is **strong**.

stuck   See **stick**.

stung   See **sting**.

submarine submarines

A **submarine** is a ship that can travel under water.

subtract subtracts, subtracting, subtracted

If you **subtract** one number from another, you take it away and count what is left. The symbol – means **subtract**, or minus.

*Three **subtract** two leaves one.* 3 – 2 = 1

subtraction

Subtraction is what you do when you take one number from another and count what is left.

succeed succeeds, succeeding, succeeded

If you **succeed**, you do what you have tried to do.

*Becky **succeeded** in getting into the team.*

suck sucks, sucking, sucked

If you **suck** something, you pull at it with your mouth.

sudden

If something is **sudden**, it happens without warning.

*The dog gave a **sudden** bark.*

suddenly

If something happens **suddenly**, you are not expecting it to happen.

*The lights **suddenly** went out.*

sugar

Sugar is used to make food and drink sweet.

suit suits

A **suit** is trousers or a skirt worn with a jacket of the same material.

suitcase suitcases

When you go on holiday, you carry your clothes in a **suitcase**.

sum sums

The **sum** of two or more numbers is what they make when you add them together.

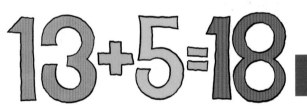

summer

Summer is the season between spring and autumn. The weather is warm and the days are long.

sun

The **sun** is a star. It shines in the sky during the day and gives us heat and light. The Earth travels around the **sun** once a year.

a b c d e f g h i j k l m n o p q r **Ss** t u v w x y z

a
b
c
d
e
f
g
h
i
j
k
l
m
n
o
p
q
r

Ss

t
u
v
w
x
y
z

Sunday Sundays

Sunday is the day of the week between Saturday and Monday.

sung See **sing**.

sunk See **sink**.

sunny sunnier, sunniest

When the weather is **sunny**, the sun is shining brightly.

sunshine

The light that comes from the sun is called **sunshine**.

supermarket supermarkets

A **supermarket** is a very large shop that sells food and other things. You take what you want as you go around and pay for it on the way out.

supper suppers

Supper is a light meal eaten in the evening.

sure

If you are **sure** that something is true, you believe it is true.

surface surfaces

The **surface** of something is the top or outside of it.

*The **surface** of the table was very shiny.*

surprise surprises, surprising, surprised

1 A **surprise** is something that you did not expect.

2 You **surprise** someone when you do something they were not expecting.

*We **surprised** my mum by taking her breakfast in bed.*

swallow swallows, swallowing, swallowed

1 When you **swallow** something, it goes down your throat and into your stomach.

2 A **swallow** is also a bird. It has a forked tail.

swam See **swim**.

swan swans

A **swan** is a very large white bird with a long curved neck. **Swans** live on rivers or lakes.

sweep sweeps, sweeping, swept

You **sweep** a floor with a brush to make it clean.

sweet **sweeter, sweetest; sweets**
1 **Sweet** food tastes of sugar.
2 A **sweet** person is friendly and loving.
3 Toffees and chocolates are **sweets**.
4 A **sweet** is also a pudding.

swept See **sweep**.

swim **swims, swimming, swam, swum**
You **swim** by using your arms and legs to move through the water.

swimming pool **swimming pools**
A **swimming pool** is a large hole in the ground that is filled with water for swimming.

swing **swings, swinging, swung**
1 A **swing** is a seat hung on chains or ropes. It moves backwards and forwards when you push it.
2 When something **swings**, it moves backwards and forwards in the air.

switch **switches**
You press on a **switch** to start a machine or turn on a light.

sword **swords**
A **sword** is a long metal blade with a handle. People fought with **swords** many years ago.

swum See **swim**.

swung See **swing**.

syllable **syllables**
A **syllable** is a word or part of a word that has one separate sound when you say it.
*"Girl" has one **syllable** and "sister" has two **syllables**.*

symbol **symbols**
A **symbol** is a letter, number or other mark that is used to mean something else.
*+ is a **symbol** that means add.*

symmetrical
If something is **symmetrical**, you can divide it into two equal and matching halves.

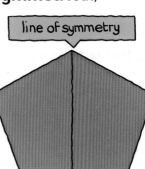

line of symmetry

symmetry
A line of **symmetry** can be drawn between the two halves of something that is symmetrical.

synonym **synonyms**
A **synonym** is a word that means the same or almost the same as another word.
(See page 180.)

syrup
Syrup is a sweet, thick liquid made by boiling sugar with water.

a b c d e f g h i j k l m n o p q r **Ss** t u v w x y z

table tables

1 A **table** is a flat surface with legs. You can work or eat at a **table**.

2 A **table** is also a way of showing information.

Day	Weather
Monday	Sunny
Tuesday	Rainy and cool
Wednesday	Showers

tadpole tadpoles

A **tadpole** is a tiny black animal that lives in water. It grows into a frog.

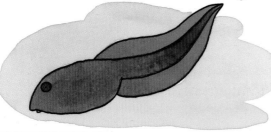

tail tails

An animal's **tail** grows at the back end of its body.

*A dog wags its **tail** when it is happy.*

take takes, taking, took, taken

1 When you **take** something, you move it from a place.
2 If you **take** one number away from another, you subtract it and count what is left. **Take away** means the same as subtract.

tale tales

A **tale** is an old word for a story.

talk talks, talking, talked

When you **talk**, you say words out loud.

tall taller, tallest

The top of a **tall** person or object is a long way from the ground.

tally tallies

If you keep a **tally**, you record the number of times something happens.

tame tamer, tamest

A **tame** animal is friendly towards humans.

*Charlotte's **tame** lamb follows her everywhere.*

tank tanks

1 A **tank** is a large container for liquids like petrol or water.
2 A **tank** is also a large fighting vehicle. It has a gun on top.

tap **taps, tapping, tapped**
1 You turn on a **tap** to run water into a sink or a bath.
2 If you **tap** something, you hit it gently.
*Mike **tapped** me on the shoulder and said hello.*

tape **tapes**
1 Tape is material in a long strip. You can use it to fasten something.
2 You can record sound or pictures onto **tape**.
*We need a new **tape** for the video recorder.*

tape measure **tape measures**
A **tape measure** is a strip of cloth or soft plastic marked into units. It is used for measuring.

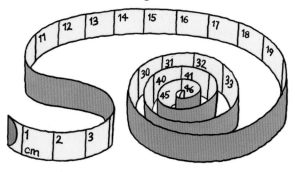

tart **tarts**
A **tart** is a round pastry case with a filling. It is often filled with fruit.

taste **tastes, tasting, tasted**
If you **taste** something, you put it in your mouth to find out what it is like to eat.

taught See **teach**.

taxi **taxis**
A **taxi** is a car that you pay to travel in.

tea
Tea is a hot drink. You make it by pouring boiling water onto dried leaves or a tea bag.

teach **teaches, teaching, taught**
If you **teach** someone, you show them how to do something.
*Can you **teach** me how to ride a bike?*

teacher **teachers**
A **teacher** helps people to learn something or shows them how to do something.

team **teams**
A **team** is a group of people who play or work together.

tear **tears, tearing, tore, torn**
1 (*sounds like* **hair**) If you **tear** something, you pull it apart.
2 (*sounds like* **here**) A **tear** is a drop of liquid that falls from your eye when you cry.

teaspoon **teaspoons**
A **teaspoon** is a small spoon used for stirring drinks.
*Add two **teaspoons** of sugar.*

teddy **teddies**
A **teddy**, or **teddy bear**, is a soft toy bear.

a
b
c
d
e
f
g
h
i
j
k
l
m
n
o
p
q
r
s
Tt
u
v
w
x
y
z

a
b
c
d
e
f
g
h
i
j
k
l
m
n
o
p
q
r
s

Tt

u
v
w
x
y
z

teeth See **tooth**.

telephone **telephones**
You use a **telephone** to speak to someone in another place.

television **televisions**
A **television** turns waves in the air into pictures and sounds. It is often called a TV.

tell **tells, telling, told**
If you **tell** someone about something, you share what you know with them.

temple **temples**
A **temple** is a place where people go to pray.

tent **tents**
You can sleep outdoors in a **tent**. It is made from a piece of cloth stretched over metal poles.

term **terms**
A school **term** is the time when you go to school between two holidays.

terrible
Something **terrible** is very frightening or nasty.
*There was a **terrible** storm last night.*

test **tests**
When you do a **test**, you answer questions to show what you can do.

text **texts**
The words in a book or poem are its **text**.

The little mouse just sat quietly and waited and waited, but nobody came. The next day

Just as he was waking up, he heard a footstep and a voice said, "Are you there, Sammy?"

thank **thanks, thanking, thanked**
You **thank** someone who has given you something or has done something for you.
***Thank** you for my new shirt, Gran!*

theatre **theatres**
You go to a **theatre** to see a show, a play or a pantomime.

theme **themes**
A **theme** of a story is the important thought that runs through it.

then
1 If something happened **then**, it happened at that time.
*We were living in our old house **then**.*
2 Then also tells you what happened next.
*First we watched a really good video, **then** we had dinner.*

thick thicker, thickest
1 If something is **thick**, it is a large distance from one side to the other.
*Jason likes **thick** bread but Katy prefers thin slices.*

2 A **thick** liquid flows slowly.

thief thieves
A **thief** is someone who steals things.

thigh thighs
Your **thigh** is the part of your leg between your knee and your hip. (See page 174.)

thin thinner, thinnest
1 Something is **thin** if there is only a short distance from one side to the other.
2 A **thin** person is not fat.

thing things
A **thing** is something that is not alive.

think thinks, thinking, thought
When you **think**, you use your brain to work something out.

thirsty thirstier, thirstiest
If you are **thirsty**, you need a drink.

thought See **think**.

thousand thousands
A **thousand** is the number 1000. It is ten hundreds.

thread threads
A **thread** is a fine string. You use it to sew things together.

threw See **throw**.

throat throats
Your **throat** is the front part of your neck.

through
If you go **through** something, you go from one side of it to the other.

throw throws, throwing, threw, thrown
When you **throw** something, you use your hand to make it travel through the air.

thumb thumbs
Your **thumb** is the short finger on the inside of your hand. (See page 174.)

thunder
Thunder is the sound that follows lightning during a storm.

thunderstorm thunderstorms
In a **thunderstorm**, there is thunder and lightning.

a b c d e f g h i j k l m n o p q r s **Tt** u v w x y z

a
b
c
d
e
f
g
h
i
j
k
l
m
n
o
p
q
r
s
Tt
u
v
w
x
y
z

Thursday Thursdays
Thursday is the day of the week between Wednesday and Friday.

tick ticks
1 A **tick** is a mark written ✔. It shows that an answer is correct.

2 The **tick** of a clock is the sound it makes every second.

ticket tickets
You buy a **ticket** to travel on a bus, train or plane. You also often need a **ticket** to go to something.
I've got two tickets for the concert.

tidy tidier, tidiest
If a room is **tidy**, everything is neat and in the right place.

tie ties, tying, tied
1 You **tie** things together by making a knot or a bow.

2 People wear a **tie** around the neck of a shirt. (See page 177.)

tiger tigers
A **tiger** is a fierce wild cat with orange fur and black stripes. **Tigers** live in Asia.

tight tighter, tightest
If something is **tight**, it fits closely.
These trousers are too tight.

tights
Tights cover your legs from your waist down to your feet. They are worn mainly by girls and women.

till
Till means until.
I'll stay till your dad comes home.

time
Seconds, minutes, hours, days, weeks, months and years are all measures of **time**. (See page 178.)

timer timers
A **timer** is a kind of clock. It can be set to measure the time left until something happens.
I've set the timer to ring after ten minutes.

times
Times is another way of saying multiplied by. The symbol × means **times**.
Three times two equals six. $3 \times 2 = 6$

tin tins
A **tin** is a small metal container. Food and paint come in **tins**.
Our dog eats a tin of dog food every day.

tiny tinier, tiniest
Something **tiny** is very small.

tip **tips**
1 A **tip** is a piece of helpful information.
2 The **tip** of something is the very end of it.
*Can you touch your nose with the **tip** of your tongue?*

tired
If you are **tired**, you need to go to sleep.

title **titles**
The **title** of a book or poem is what the writer has called it.
*The **title** of this book is Collins First School Dictionary.*

toad **toads**
A **toad** is an animal like a large frog.

toast
Toast is a slice of bread that is cooked until it is light brown. It is often eaten with butter.

today
Today is the day you are in now.
*It is my birthday **today**.*

toe **toes**
You have five **toes** on the end of each foot. (See page 174.)

toffee **toffees**
Toffee is a chewy sweet.

toilet **toilets**
You go to the **toilet** to empty waste from your body.

told See **tell**.

tomato **tomatoes**
A **tomato** is a red fruit. You often eat it raw.

tomorrow
Tomorrow is the day that comes after today.

tongue **tongues**
Your **tongue** is inside your mouth. You use it when you speak or eat.
*My sister likes to stick out her **tongue**.*

tongue twister
tongue twisters
A **tongue twister** is difficult to say quickly and correctly.
*"Red lorry, yellow lorry" is a well-known **tongue twister**.*

tonight
Tonight means the end of today.
*Will you come with me to the match **tonight**?*

took See **take**.

tool **tools**
You use a **tool** to make or fix things.
*My dad uses special **tools** when he repairs the car.*

a
b
c
d
e
f
g
h
i
j
k
l
m
n
o
p
q
r
s
Tt
u
v
w
x
y
z

a
b
c
d
e
f
g
h
i
j
k
l
m
n
o
p
q
r
s

Tt

u
v
w
x
y
z

tooth **teeth**
You have hard, white, bony **teeth** inside your mouth. You use them when you chew or bite.

toothbrush **toothbrushes**
You use a **toothbrush** to clean your teeth.

toothpaste
You spread **toothpaste** on a toothbrush when you clean your teeth.

top **tops**
The **top** of something is its highest part.
They climbed to the very top of the mountain.

torch **torches**
A **torch** is a light you can carry.

tore See **tear**.

torn See **tear**.

tortoise **tortoises**
A **tortoise** is a reptile with a shell on its back. It moves very slowly.

toss **tosses, tossing, tossed**
When you **toss** something, you throw it in the air.

total **totals**
When you add things up, you work out their **total**.

touch **touches, touching, touched**
1 When you **touch** something, you put your hand on it.
2 When things **touch**, they are placed against each other.

tough **tougher, toughest**
Tough means very strong and not easily broken.

tow **tows, towing, towed**
If you **tow** something, you pull it along behind you.
The car towed a caravan.

towel **towels**
You dry yourself with a **towel**.

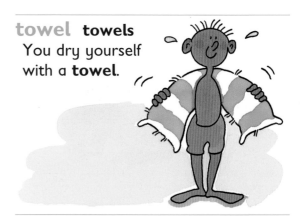

tower **towers**
A **tower** is a tall building. It is often part of another building.

town **towns**
A **town** is a collection of homes and businesses. It is larger than a village and smaller than a city.

toy **toys**
A **toy** is something that you play with for fun.

trace **traces, tracing, traced**
When you **trace** something, you make a copy by drawing over it through a piece of clear paper.

track **tracks**

1 A **track** is a path for people or animals.

2 Railway trains run on **track** made from long strips of metal.

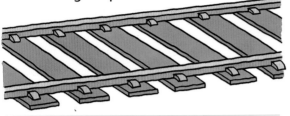

tractor **tractors**

A **tractor** is a vehicle that is used on a farm.

traffic

Traffic is all the vehicles on the roads at one time.

traffic light **traffic lights**

Traffic lights tell traffic when to go or stop. They are red, yellow and green.

trail **trails**

A **trail** is a path or marks that you can follow.

train **trains**

A **train** is an engine and carriages that run on railway track.

trap **traps, trapping, trapped**

If you are **trapped**, you are in a place that you cannot get out of.

travel **travels, travelling, travelled**

When you **travel**, you go on a journey.

treasure **treasures**

A **treasure** is something valuable.

tree **trees**

A **tree** is a large plant. It has a wooden trunk and branches with leaves on.

triangle **triangles**

A **triangle** is a flat shape with three sides.

triangular

Anything in the shape of a triangle is **triangular**.

trick **tricks, tricking, tricked**

1 If you **trick** someone, you make them believe something that is not true.

2 A **trick** is also a piece of magic.

tried See **try**.

tries See **try**.

trim **trims, trimming, trimmed**

If you **trim** something, you cut it to make it neat and tidy.

*Dad is **trimming** the hedge.*

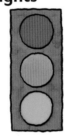

a
b
c
d
e
f
g
h
i
j
k
l
m
n
o
p
q
r
s

Tt

u
v
w
x
y
z

trip trips, tripping, tripped

1 If you **trip** over something, you catch your foot on it and fall over.
2 If you go on a **trip**, you travel somewhere.
Lou is going on a trip to a museum.

trolley trolleys

A **trolley** has wheels and a handle. You use it to move heavy things.

trouble

1 You get into **trouble** if you do something wrong.
If I'm late home I'll get into trouble.
2 If you have **trouble**, you have a problem.

trousers

You wear **trousers** to cover your body from your waist to your ankles. **Trousers** have separate legs.

truck trucks

A **truck** is a short, heavy vehicle. It is used for carrying things.

true truer, truest

If something is **true**, it really happened.

trumpet trumpets

A **trumpet** is a musical instrument made of metal. You blow through it to make a sound.

trunk trunks

1 The part of a tree that grows up from the ground is called a **trunk**.
2 An elephant's long nose is called a **trunk**.

trust trusts, trusting, trusted

If you **trust** someone, you believe they will do what they say.

truth

When you tell the **truth**, you say what really happened.

try tries, trying, tried

When you **try** to do something, you do it as well as you can.

T-shirt T-shirts

A **T-shirt** is a soft cotton shirt with short sleeves and no collar.

tube tubes

A **tube** is a hollow cylinder.

tuck tucks, tucking, tucked

1 If you **tuck** someone in, you make them comfortable in bed.
2 When you **tuck** into food, you start to eat it.

Tuesday Tuesdays

Tuesday is the day of the week between Monday and Wednesday.

tug-of-war

A **tug-of-war** is a contest. Two teams pull on the ends of a rope. The winners pull the other side over the winning line.

tumble   **tumbles, tumbling, tumbled**

You **tumble** when you fall head over heels.

*Jack fell down and Jill came **tumbling** after him.*

tummy   **tummies**

Tummy is another word for stomach. When you swallow your food, it goes into your **tummy**.

tune   **tunes**

A **tune** is the notes that go together to make a piece of music.

*That song has a **tune** that is easy to remember.*

tunnel   **tunnels**

A **tunnel** is a long hole through the ground.

turn   **turns, turning, turned**

1 When you **turn**, you move to your left or your right.
2 If people take **turns**, they do something one after another.
3 If something **turns** into something else, it changes.

*Water **turns** into ice when it freezes.*

turnip   **turnips**

A **turnip** is a round vegetable that is white or yellow inside.

tusk   **tusks**

A **tusk** is a large horn on the head of an elephant or rhinoceros.

TV   **TVs**

TV is short for television.

twice

Twice means two times.
*Knock **twice** and then wait.*
Twice 3 is 6.

twig   **twigs**

A **twig** is a small branch of a tree or bush.

twin   **twins**

When a mother has **twins**, she has two babies at the same time. **Twins** often look alike.

twist   **twists, twisting, twisted**

When you **twist** something, you bend it into a round shape.

tying   See **tie**.

type   **types, typing, typed**

1 When you **type** something, you use a keyboard to print letters.
2 A **type** is one kind of a thing.
*What **type** of shoes do you like best?*

tyre   **tyres**

A **tyre** is a piece of thick rubber that goes round a wheel.

a b c d e f g h i j k l m n o p q r s **Tt** u v w x y z

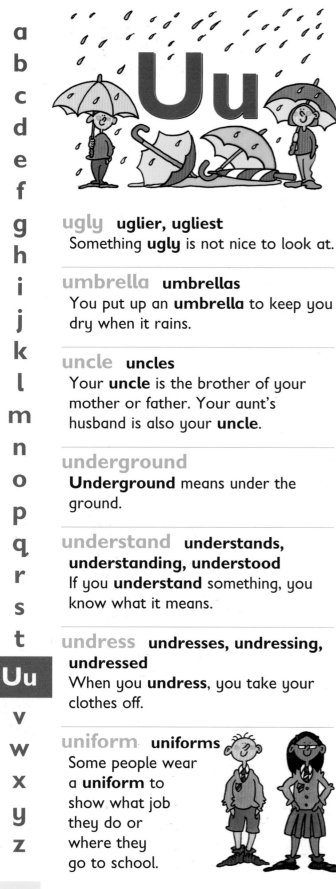

ugly uglier, ugliest
Something **ugly** is not nice to look at.

umbrella umbrellas
You put up an **umbrella** to keep you dry when it rains.

uncle uncles
Your **uncle** is the brother of your mother or father. Your aunt's husband is also your **uncle**.

underground
Underground means under the ground.

understand understands, understanding, understood
If you **understand** something, you know what it means.

undress undresses, undressing, undressed
When you **undress**, you take your clothes off.

uniform uniforms
Some people wear a **uniform** to show what job they do or where they go to school.

unit units
The **units** of a number are the ones. *The number 37 has three tens and seven* **units**.

universe
The **universe** is space and all the stars and planets.

until
Until a time means finishing then.

upset
If you are **upset**, you are sad and may feel like crying.

upside down
If something is **upside down**, its top is where its bottom should be.

upstairs
If you go **upstairs**, you go up to a higher level of a building.

urgent
Something **urgent** must be done at once.

use uses, using, used
Something is **used** to do a job.

useful
Something **useful** is used to do a job.

usual
Something **usual** happens most of the time.

usually
Usually means often but not always.

vacuum cleaner

vacuum cleaners
A **vacuum cleaner**
is a machine
that sucks
up dust.

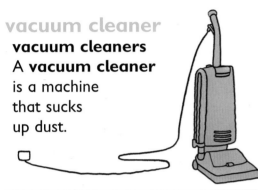

valley   valleys

A **valley** is a low area of land
between hills or mountains.

valuable

Something **valuable** is worth a lot of
money.
The thief stole a valuable clock.

van   vans

A **van** is a vehicle for carrying things.

vanish   vanishes, vanishing, vanished

If something **vanishes**, you suddenly
cannot see it any more.
*I had my pencil a minute ago but now it's
vanished!*

vase   vases

You put flowers
in a **vase**.

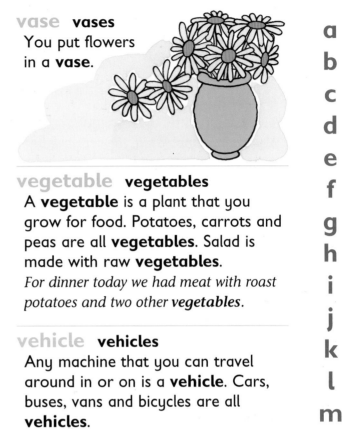

vegetable   vegetables

A **vegetable** is a plant that you
grow for food. Potatoes, carrots and
peas are all **vegetables**. Salad is
made with raw **vegetables**.
*For dinner today we had meat with roast
potatoes and two other vegetables.*

vehicle   vehicles

Any machine that you can travel
around in or on is a **vehicle**. Cars,
buses, vans and bicycles are all
vehicles.

verb   verbs

A **verb** is a word that says what is
happening or being done.

The birds sang
as Patrick walked to school.
verbs

verse   verses

A **verse** is a group of lines of a poem
or a song, like this:
*Here we go round the mulberry bush,
The mulberry bush, the mulberry bush,
Here we go round the mulberry bush,
On a cold and frosty morning.*

a b c d e f g h i j k l m n o p q r s t u **Vv** w x y z

a
b
c
d
e
f
g
h
i
j
k
l
m
n
o
p
q
r
s
t
u

Vv

w
x
y
z

vest vests
A **vest** is a piece of clothing. It is worn under a shirt.

vet vets
A **vet** looks after sick animals.
*When our puppy was ill, the **vet** gave her some pills to make her better.*

video videos, videoing, videoed
1 A **video** is a tape with TV programmes or films recorded on it. You play a **video** on a **video** recorder and watch it on a television.
2 If you **video** something, you record pictures and sounds on tape.
3 A **video** camera records moving pictures and sound.

village villages
A **village** is a group of streets and houses. It is smaller than a town.

violin violins
A **violin** is a musical instrument made of wood. You play it by holding it under your chin and pulling a stick called a bow across the strings.

visible
If something is **visible**, you can see it.
*I'm just **visible** behind my mum in this photo.*

visit visits, visiting, visited
When you **visit** someone, you go to see them at their home.

visitor visitors
A **visitor** is someone who comes to visit you.
*We've got **visitors** coming to stay this weekend.*

voice voices
Your **voice** is the sound you make when you speak.
*I caught a bad cold and lost my **voice**.*

volcano volcanoes
A **volcano** is a mountain that sometimes throws smoke and melted rocks into the sky.

vote votes, voting, voted
You **vote** for someone or something by saying which you choose.
*We **voted** to buy a hamster as a class pet.*

vowel vowels
The **vowels** are the letters a, e, i, o and u. The other letters are consonants.

Ww

wagon **wagons**
A **wagon** is used to carry heavy things. It is usually pulled by horses.

waist **waists**
Your **waist** is the middle part of your body. (See page 174.)

wait **waits, waiting, waited**
If you **wait** for something, you don't do something until it happens.
*I am **waiting** for Kyle to help me.*

wake **wakes, waking, woke, woken**
You **wake** up when you stop being asleep.

walk **walks, walking, walked**
You **walk** by putting one foot in front of the other. **Walking** is slower than running.

wall **walls**
A **wall** of a building or room is one of its sides.
*I'll hang your picture on the **wall**.*

wand **wands**
A magician or wizard uses a small stick called a **wand** when they do magic tricks.

want **wants, wanting, wanted**
If you **want** something, you would like to have it.
*Bethany **wants** a banana.*

war **wars**
When countries go to **war**, their armies fight each other.

wardrobe **wardrobes**
A **wardrobe** is a large cupboard for keeping clothes in.

warm **warmer, warmest**
Warm means quite hot but not very hot.
*This bread is still **warm** from the oven.*

warn **warns, warning, warned**
You **warn** someone by telling them about something bad that might happen.
*The weather man **warned** us of storms and rain.*

warning **warnings**
A **warning** tells you that there is something bad or dangerous.
*The notice said: "**Warning**: fog".*

wash **washes, washing, washed**
You **wash** yourself with water to make your skin clean.

washing machine
washing machines
A **washing machine** is a machine that washes clothes.

a b c d e f g h i j k l m n o p q r s t u v

Ww

x y z

a
b
c
d
e
f
g
h
i
j
k
l
m
n
o
p
q
r
s
t
u
v

Ww

x
y
z

wasp wasps

A **wasp** is an insect with black and yellow stripes. It has a sting.

waste wastes, wasting, wasted

When you **waste** something, you do not use it well.

*You've **wasted** an hour finding your pen.*
*This food will be **wasted** if no one eats it.*

watch watches, watching, watched

1 A **watch** is a small clock you wear on your wrist.

2 You **watch** someone by looking at them to see what they are doing.

water

Water falls from the sky as rain. It flows down rivers to the sea.

waterproof

If something is **waterproof**, it does not let in water.

*Bring a **waterproof** coat in case it rains.*

wave waves, waving, waved

1 You **wave** to someone by raising your arm and moving it about.

2 A **wave** is also a raised line of water that moves across the sea.

*The surfer rode on a huge **wave**.*

wax

Wax is a material. It is used to make candles and crayons. **Wax** melts when it is heated.

way ways

1 If you tell someone the **way**, you say how to get to a place.

2 The **way** to do something is how to do it.

*This is the **way** to throw the ball.*

weak weaker, weakest

Weak means not strong.

*I ran up the hill till my legs felt **weak**.*

wear wears, wearing, wore, worn

1 When you **wear** clothes, you have them on.

*Ryan's **wearing** jeans today.*

2 When something is **worn** out, it cannot be used any more.

weather

Rain, sunshine, storms and snow are different kinds of **weather**.

*What's the **weather** like today?*

web webs

A spider makes a **web** using threads that it makes in its body.

*Spiders make **webs** to trap insects.*

website websites

You look at a **website** on the Internet to find information.

wedding weddings

When two people get married, it is their **wedding** day.

Wednesday **Wednesdays**
Wednesday is the day of the week between Tuesday and Thursday.

weed **weeds**
A **weed** is a wild plant that people do not want in their gardens.

week **weeks**
A **week** is made up of seven days. There are 52 **weeks** in a year.

weekend **weekends**
Saturday and Sunday are called the **weekend**.

weigh **weighs, weighing, weighed**
Something that **weighs** a lot is hard to lift or carry. *An elephant weighs much more than a mouse.*

weight
The **weight** of something is how much it weighs.

well **better, best; wells**
1 If you do something **well**, you make a good job of it.
2 If you are **well**, you are healthy.
3 People get water out of a deep hole in the ground called a **well**.

wellington or **welly** **wellingtons or wellies**
Wellingtons are rubber boots. They keep your feet and legs dry.

went See **go**.

west
West is the direction you look when you see the sun set.

wet **wetter, wettest**
1 Something that is **wet** has water or liquid on it.
2 If the weather is **wet**, it is raining.

whale **whales**
Whales are the largest mammals. They live in the sea.

what
What is used to ask or talk about a thing.
*What is that? I can't see **what** it is.*

wheat
Wheat is a plant grown by farmers. Flour is made from its seeds.

wheel **wheels**
Cars, lorries and bicycles move along on **wheels**.

wheelchair **wheelchairs**
A **wheelchair** is a chair with wheels. It is used by someone who cannot walk.

when
When means the time at which something happens.
When are we going to the match?

a
b
c
d
e
f
g
h
i
j
k
l
m
n
o
p
q
r
s
t
u
v

Ww

x
y
z

a
b
c
d
e
f
g
h
i
j
k
l
m
n
o
p
q
r
s
t
u
v

Ww

x
y
z

where
Where means the place at which something is.
Where is my bag? It isn't where I left it.

which
Which means the thing you have in mind.
Which book have you chosen? Show me which one you like best.

while
While means that two things happen at the same time.
We went skating while we were in France.

whisper   whispers, whispering, whispered
If you **whisper**, you speak very quietly.

whistle   whistles, whistling, whistled
1 You **whistle** by blowing air out of your mouth very loudly.
2 You can make the same noise using a metal or plastic **whistle**.

who
Who is used to ask or talk about a person.
Who put this frog on my chair?
I'm the person who telephoned you yesterday.

whole
The **whole** of something means every part of it.
Janice ate the whole cake by herself.

whose
Whose is used to ask or talk about the person something belongs to.
Whose pencils are these?
She's the girl whose mother is a singer.

why
Why is used to ask or talk about the reason for something.
Why are your shoelaces undone?
That's why you fell over!

wicked
A **wicked** person is evil. They do **wicked** things that are very unkind.

wide   wider, widest
Something **wide** measures a long way from side to side.

width
When you measure how wide something is, you find its **width**.

wife   wives
A **wife** is a woman that a man is married to.
My gran is my grandad's wife.

wild   wilder, wildest
A **wild** animal or flower is one that lives without help from humans.

win **wins, winning, won**
The person who **wins** comes first in a race or competition.
*My team **won** the swimming race.*

wind **winds**
Wind is air that moves strongly and quickly.

windmill **windmills**
A **windmill** is a tower with large arms that are moved around by the wind. Farmers used to use power from a **windmill** to make flour.

window **windows**
A **window** is a hole in the wall that lets in light. **Windows** are often filled with glass.

windscreen **windscreens**
The driver of a car looks out through the **windscreen**. (See page 175.)

windy **windier, windiest**
It is **windy** when the wind is blowing more strongly than usual.

wing **wings**
A bird flaps its **wings** to help it to fly. An aeroplane's **wings** are fixed.

winner **winners**
The person who wins something is the **winner**.
*The **winner** of the first prize is Alfie.*

winter
Winter is the season between autumn and spring. It is cold and the days are short.

wipe **wipes, wiping, wiped**
If you **wipe** something, you clean it with paper or a cloth.
*Hayley is **wiping** the table.*

wire **wires**
A **wire** is a long, thin strip of metal. It bends easily and is used to fasten things. Fences and baskets can be made of **wire**.

wise **wiser, wisest**
A **wise** person knows a lot and is very sensible.

wish **wishes, wishing, wished**
1 If you **wish** for something, you want it very much.
2 When you make a **wish**, you hope to get what you want.

witch **witches**
A **witch** is a woman in stories who can do magic.

wives See **wife**.

a
b
c
d
e
f
g
h
i
j
k
l
m
n
o
p
q
r
s
t
u
v
Ww
x
y
z

167

a
b
c
d
e
f
g
h
i
j
k
l
m
n
o
p
q
r
s
t
u
v

Ww

x
y
z

wizard **wizards**
A **wizard** is a man in stories who can do magic.

wobble **wobbles, wobbling, wobbled**
If something **wobbles**, it shakes from side to side.
The jelly wobbled on the plate.

wobbly
If something is **wobbly**, it wobbles.

woke See **wake**.

woken See **wake**.

wolf **wolves**
A **wolf** is a wild animal like a large dog. **Wolves** live in groups called packs.

woman **women**
A **woman** is a grown-up female person.

won See **win**.

wonder **wonders, wondering, wondered**
When you **wonder** about something, you think about if it will happen.
I wonder if Gran will come today.

wonderful
Something **wonderful** is very good.
We've got a wonderful new TV!

won't
Won't is a short way of saying "will not".

wood **woods**
1 **Wood** is the material that comes from the trunks of trees.
2 A **wood** is a large group of trees.

wooden
Wooden means made from wood.

wool
A sheep's coat is made of **wool**. **Wool** is used to make clothes and blankets.

word **words**
You use **words** when you speak or write. A written **word** is a group of letters. It has a space at each side.

wore See **wear**.

work **works, working, worked**
1 Someone who **works** tries hard to do something.
2 When someone goes to **work**, they are going to do their job.

world **worlds**
The **world** is the planet that you live on and everything on it.

worm **worms**
A **worm** is a small slippery animal. It lives in the soil.

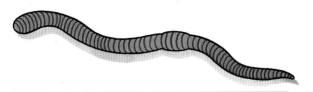

worn See **wear**.

worry **worries, worrying, worried**
If you **worry** about something, you are afraid that it might go wrong.

worse
Worse means more bad.
This film is even worse than last week's!
See **bad**.

worst
Worst means most bad.
This is the worst film I have ever watched!
See **bad**.

worth
1 Something is **worth** what you would expect to pay for it.
2 Something that is **worth** doing has a good result.

wound **wounds**
A **wound** is a cut or break in the skin.

wrap **wraps, wrapping, wrapped**
When you **wrap** something, you put something around it to cover it.

wriggle **wriggles, wriggling, wriggled**
If you **wriggle,** you move your body quickly from side to side.

wrinkle **wrinkles**
A **wrinkle** is a small fold.
Look at the wrinkles on that elephant!

wrist **wrists**
Your **wrist** is the place where your hand joins your arm. (See page 174.)

write **writes, writing, wrote, written**
You **write** when you put words on paper with a pen or pencil.

writing
When you have done some **writing**, you have written words on paper.

written See **write**.

wrong
1 Something **wrong** is not correct.
2 **Wrong** also means against the rules that people have made.
Telling lies is wrong.

wrote See **write**.

a
b
c
d
e
f
g
h
i
j
k
l
m
n
o
p
q
r
s
t
u
v
Ww
x
y
z

X-ray X-rays

An **X-ray** is a photograph of the inside of your body. It is taken using a special kind of light.

xylophone xylophones

A **xylophone** is a musical instrument. You play it by hitting wooden bars with sticks.

yacht yachts

A **yacht** is a sailing boat. People sail **yachts** for fun.

yawn yawns, yawning, yawned

You **yawn** by opening your mouth wide and breathing out noisily. You **yawn** when you are tired.

Tom yawned and said he was going to bed.

year years

A **year** has 365 days. There are twelve months in a **year**.

yell yells, yelling, yelled

You **yell** when you shout as loudly as you can.

The children were yelling with excitement.

yes

You say **yes** to show that you agree with something or that someone is right.

"I really like ice cream!" "Yes, so do I!"
"This is your coat, isn't it?" "Yes, it is."

yesterday

Yesterday was the day that came before today.

yogurt or yoghurt yogurts or yoghurts

Yogurt is a soft, thick food made from milk. It is often mixed with sugar or fruit.

yolk yolks
The **yolk** of an egg is the yellow part in the middle.

young younger, youngest
A **young** person or animal has not been alive for long.

your
Your means belonging to you.
*Is this **your** coat?*

yo-yo yo-yos
A **yo-yo** is a toy that goes up and down on a string.

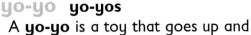

zero zeroes
Zero is a name for the number 0.

zigzag zigzags
A **zigzag** is a line that bends suddenly up and down.

zebra zebras
A **zebra** is an animal that lives in Africa. It is like a small horse with black and white stripes.

zebra crossing
zebra crossings
A **zebra crossing** is a place to cross the road. There are black and white stripes on the road.

zip zips
A **zip** is a line of teeth that lock together to close something.

zoo zoos
Animals are kept in a **zoo** so that people can look at them.

a
b
c
d
e
f
g
h
i
j
k
l
m
n
o
p
q
r
s
t
u
v
w
x
Yy
Zz

Dinosaurs

Brontosaurus was a
plant-eating dinosaur with
a long neck and long tail.

Tyrannosaurus rex was one of the
largest meat-eaters, with very sharp
teeth and claws.

Triceratops used its three horns to
fight off other dinosaurs.

Pterodactyl lived at the same time
as the dinosaurs.

Stegosaurus had bony plates on its back and a spiky tail to protect it.

Parts of the body

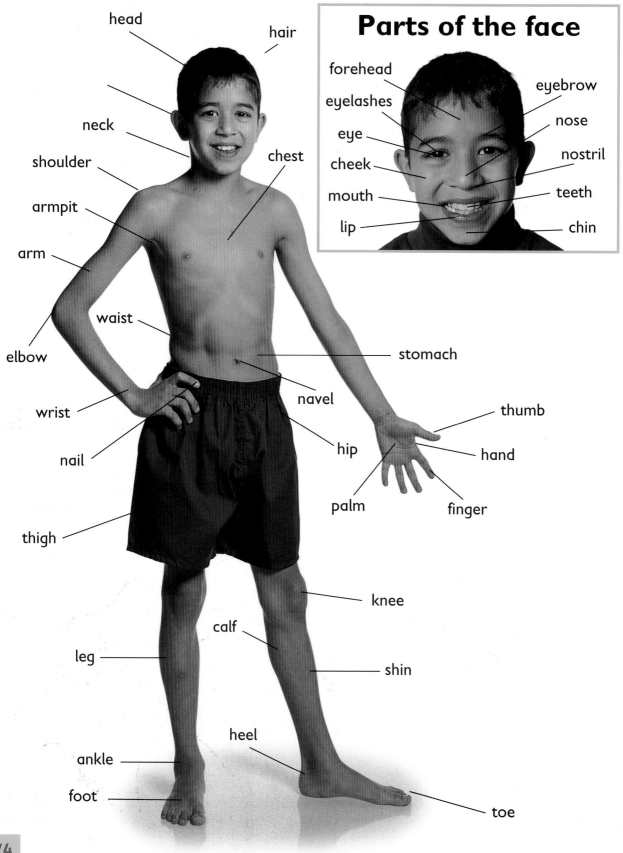

head

hair

Parts of the face

forehead

eyebrow

eyelashes

nose

eye

nostril

cheek

neck

teeth

mouth

shoulder

chin

lip

chest

armpit

arm

waist

stomach

elbow

navel

thumb

wrist

hip

hand

nail

palm

finger

thigh

knee

calf

leg

shin

heel

ankle

foot

toe

Parts of a bicycle

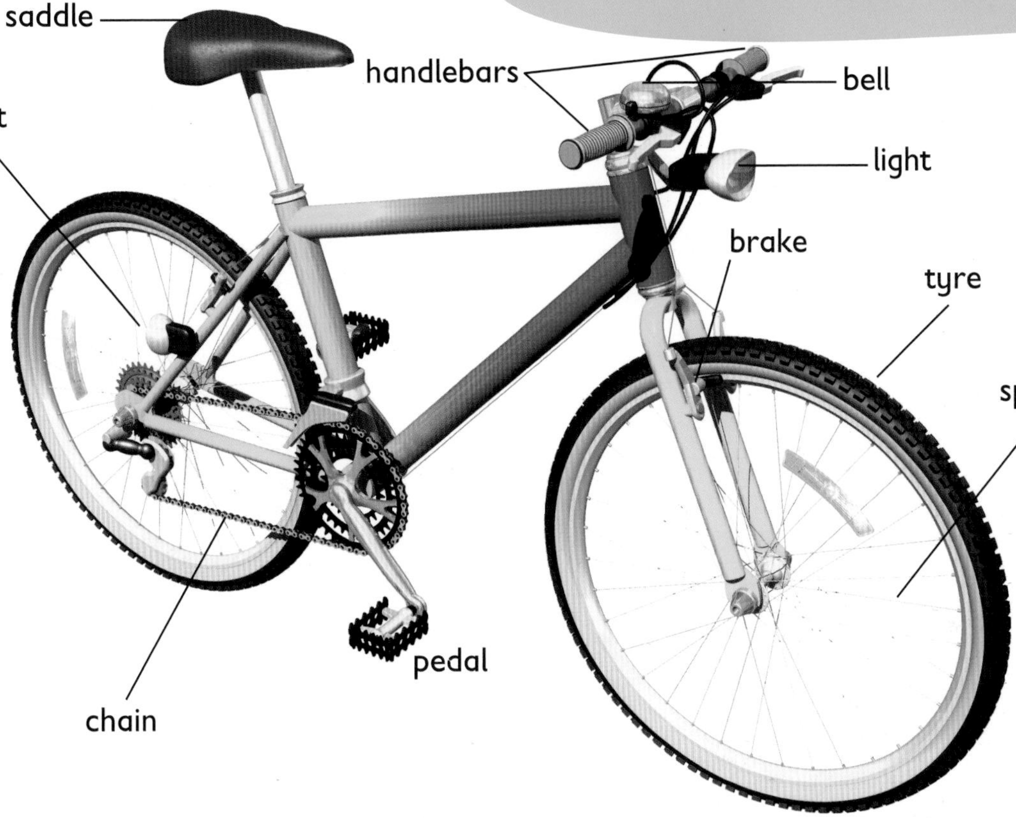

saddle

handlebars

bell

light

light

brake

tyre

spoke

wheel

chain

pedal

Parts of a car

roof

windscreen

windscreen
wiper

bonnet

boot

petrol
cap

engine

headlight

rear door

front door

door handle

tyre

bumper

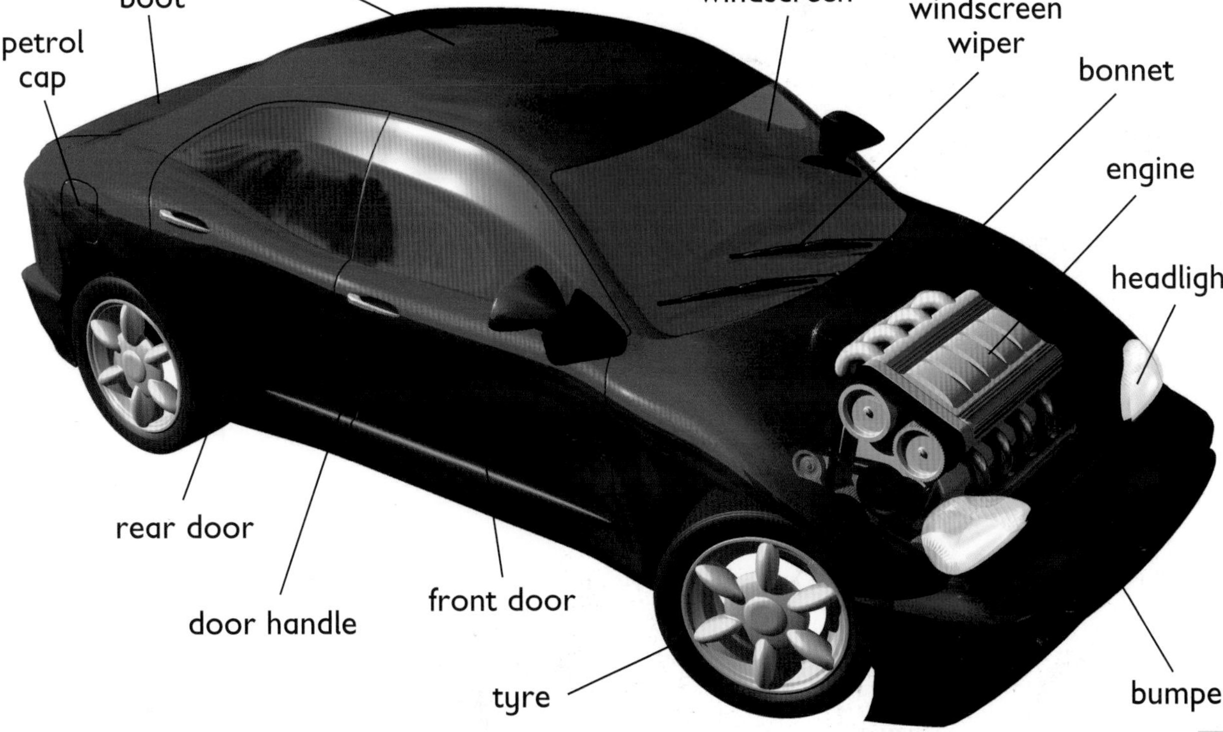

Clothes

blouse

scarf

dressing gown

nightdress

hat

jumper

jacket

skirt

glove

sandals

jeans

coat

tights

trainers

dress

swimsuit

slippers

knickers

leotard

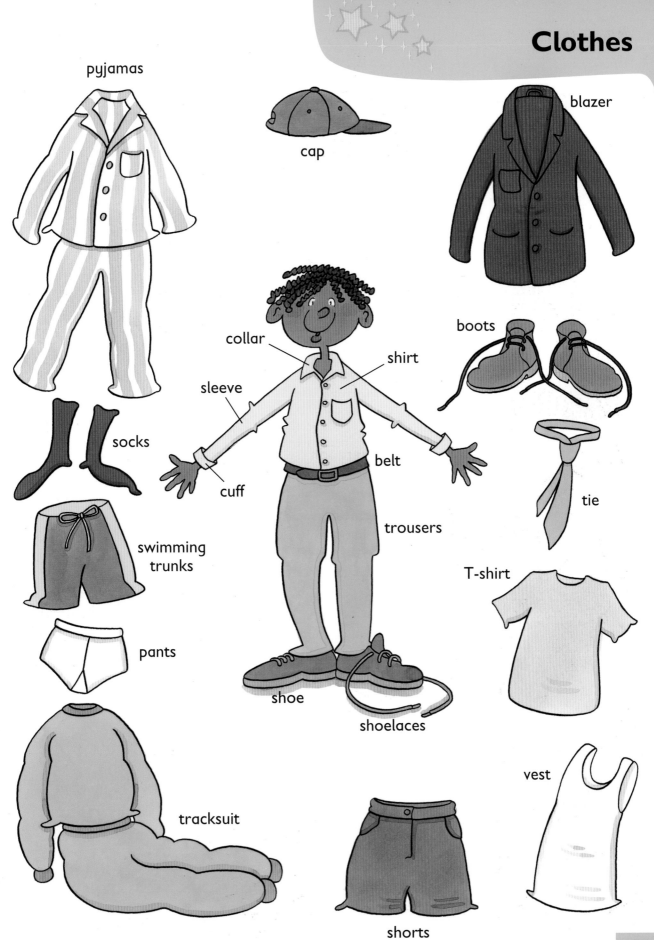

Clothes

pyjamas

cap

blazer

collar

sleeve

shirt

boots

socks

cuff

belt

tie

swimming trunks

trousers

pants

T-shirt

shoe

shoelaces

vest

tracksuit

shorts

Time

one o'clock

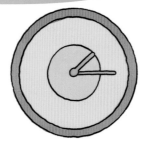
quarter past one

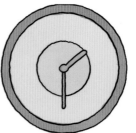
half past one

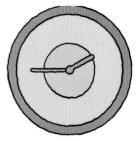
quarter to two

1:00

1:15

1:30

1:45

yesterday
today
tomorrow

second
minute
hour
day
week
fortnight
month
year
decade
century
millennium

dawn
morning
midday
noon
afternoon
dusk
evening
night
midnight

Days
Monday
Tuesday
Wednesday
Thursday
Friday
Saturday
Sunday

Months
January
February
March
April
May
June
July
August
September
October
November
December

Seasons

spring

summer

autumn

winter

how   what   when   where   who   why   which

Pronouns

I	me	my	mine	myself
you	you	your	yours	yourself, yourselves
he, she, it	him, her, it	his, her, its	his, hers, its	himself, herself, itself
we	us	our	ours	ourselves
they	them	their	theirs	themselves

Words we use a lot

a	can't	like	should
about	come	look	so
after	could	many	some
again	did	may	than
all	do	more	that
am	don't	much	the
an	for	must	then
and	from	next	there
another	get	no	these
are	go	not	this
as	going	now	to
at	got	of	too
away	had	once	very
back	has	or	was
be	have	out	way
because	here	play	went
been	if	put	were
but	in	said	will
by	into	saw	with
came	is	see	would
can	just	seen	yes

Synonyms

Synonyms are words that have almost the same meaning.

How many synonyms can you think of?

small
tiny ...

big
large ...

tasty
delicious ...

neat
tidy ...

wet
damp ...

unhappy
sad ...

yell
shout ...

cook
bake ...

afraid
scared ...

fast
quick ...

18+7=25

Antonyms

Antonyms are words that mean the opposite.

high   low

wide   narrow

hot   cold

sad   happy

old

new

come

go

asleep   awake

full   empty

dark   light

inside   outside

open   closed

back   front

heavy   light

few

many

noisy   quiet

clean   dirty

soft   hard

wet   dry

fast   slow

Position words

up

down

top

first

bottom

through

above

below

between

last

on

off

far

over

beside

behind

under

near

in front

Numbers

0	zero	21	twenty-one	1st	first
1	one	30	thirty	2nd	second
2	two	31	thirty-one	3rd	third
3	three	40	forty	4th	fourth
4	four	41	forty-one	5th	fifth
5	five	50	fifty	6th	sixth
6	six	51	fifty-one	7th	seventh
7	seven	60	sixty	8th	eighth
8	eight	61	sixty-one	9th	ninth
9	nine	70	seventy	10th	tenth
10	ten	71	seventy-one	11th	eleventh
11	eleven	80	eighty	12th	twelfth
12	twelve	81	eighty-one	13th	thirteenth
13	thirteen	90	ninety	14th	fourteenth
14	fourteen	91	ninety-one	15th	fifteenth
15	fifteen	100	one hundred	16th	sixteenth
16	sixteen	200	two hundred	17th	seventeenth
17	seventeen	1000	one thousand	18th	eighteenth
18	eighteen	10 000	ten thousand	19th	nineteenth
19	nineteen	100 000	one hundred thousand	20th	twentieth
20	twenty	1 000 000	one million	21st	twenty-first

Measurement

Length
millimetre (mm)
centimetre (cm)
metre (m)
kilometre (km)

Mass
gram (g)
half-kilogram
kilogram (kg)

Capacity
millilitre (ml)
half-litre
litre (l)

Shapes and colours

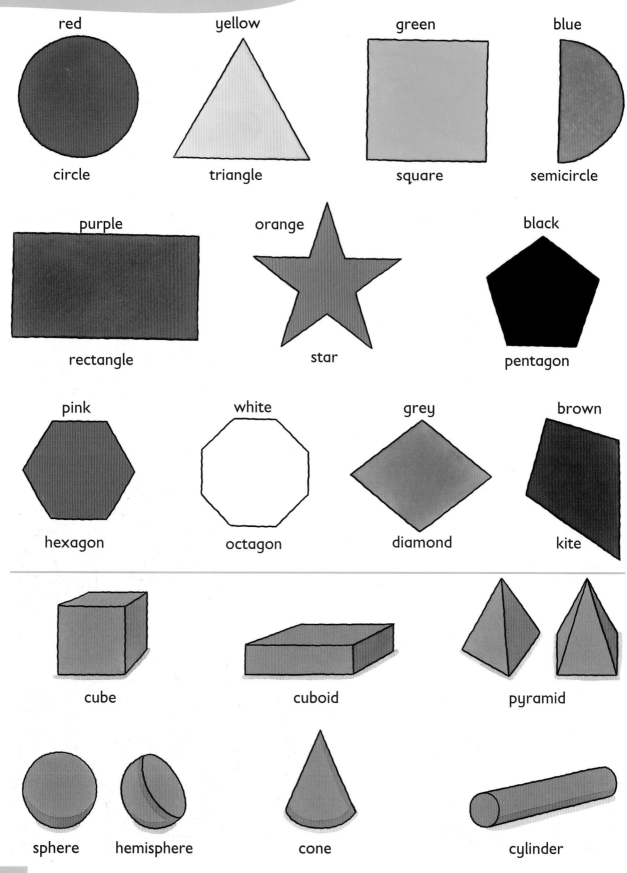

red
circle

yellow
triangle

green
square

blue
semicircle

purple
rectangle

orange
star

black
pentagon

pink
hexagon

white
octagon

grey
diamond

brown
kite

cube

cuboid

pyramid

sphere

hemisphere

cone

cylinder

Plural means more than one. You can find out how to make a plural by using your dictionary. Look up the word you want and you will find the plural beside it, like this.

lemon **lemons**
A **lemon** is a small yellow fruit. It has a very sharp flavour.

? These pictures all show more than one thing. Write down the plural words. Remember to check the endings. Use your dictionary to see if you were right.

1

2

3

4

5

6
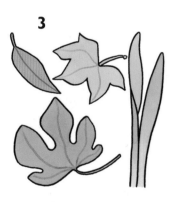

7
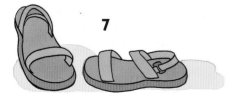

8

Word jumble

? The letters in these words are jumbled up. Try to unjumble them, then check the spelling in the dictionary.

hothguesil

shipomopatup

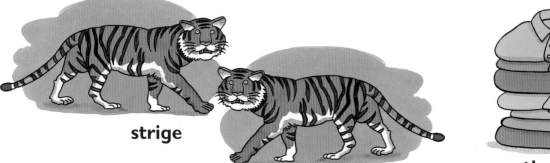

strige

thsisr

ipg uiagen

summohors

arbsze

ulbl

Word Wizard quiz

? Look at these pictures one by one. Then look at the question.
Look the word up in the dictionary to find the answer.

1 Where can you sleep in a ?

2 How many colours are there in a ?

3 Who travels in a ?

4 What do we use to make a ?

5 What comes from a ?

6 How do you make a cup of ?

7 Where does a wild live ?

8 What is the wide part of a called ?

9 What is an made of ?

10 How often does the go around the Earth ?

Sound detectives!

? The words in each group have some letters missing. Can you work out what they are? (**Top tip**: try saying the words aloud!)

1
g _ _ l   b _ _ d   sk _ _ t

2
b _ _ nstalk

b _ _ k

b _ _ ch

3
c _ _ ch

g _ _ t   b _ _ t

4
_ _ ch   _ _ m   f _ _ m

5
be _ _   ba _ _   windmi _ _

? Look at these groups of pictures. Each group belongs together for a reason. Can you work out what the reason is? (**Top tip**: try saying the name of each picture aloud!)

Answer The words in each group rhyme.

A-Z challenge

? Put the pictures in each group into alphabetical order. (**Top tip**: writing the words down will help!)

1

2

3

4

Write a story

Have you ever thought about writing a story of your own? It's easier than you think! Here are some ideas on how to get started.

Think of the place you want to set your story.

Think of the people you want to have in your story.

Think of what you'd like the people to do.

Storyboard

Now think of a story using the things shown in these pictures. You can use them in any order you like.

Weblinks

What is the Internet?

The Internet is a large group of computers that are all linked together.

How to use the Internet

You find things on the Internet by using something called a **search engine**.

Ask a teacher, parent or carer to help you go online and find the search engine. You will see a box on the screen that you can type in. Enter the name of the thing you want to find out about. Make sure you spell it correctly! Then click "search". The search engine will show you lots of websites.

There are sites full of exciting and interesting things just for children, but make sure you ask an adult to help you find them. For instance, you can find out about…

people from days
gone by

wild animals

dinosaurs

Staying safe

You wouldn't go out to play without telling your parents or carers where you were going! In the same way, make sure that you take care while you're using the Internet.

- ★ Always make sure that your parents or carers know that you're using the Internet.
- ★ Never give out any personal information, such as your name address, over the Internet.

- ★ Never go to meet anyone you've met online without being accompanied by a parent or carer.

To find out more about websites that will be fun to use, go to

www.collins.co.uk/word_wizard

NEWFIELDS PRIMARY SCHOOL